Agile Project Management and Complexity

A Reappraisal

Czesław Mesjasz, Katarzyna Bartusik, Tomasz Małkus and Mariusz Sołtysik

Routledge
Taylor & Francis Group
LONDON AND NEW YORK

First published 2022
by Routledge
4 Park Square, Milton Park, Abingdon, Oxon OX14 4RN

and by Routledge
605 Third Avenue, New York, NY 10158

Routledge is an imprint of the Taylor & Francis Group, an informa business

British Library Cataloguing-in-Publication Data
A catalogue record for this book is available from the British Library

Library of Congress Cataloging-in-Publication Data
A catalog record has been requested for this book

ISBN: 978-1-032-00652-9 (hbk)
ISBN: 978-1-032-00654-3 (pbk)
ISBN: 978-1-003-17503-2 (ebk)

DOI: 10.4324/9781003175032

Typeset in Bembo
by Deanta Global Publishing Services, Chennai, India

Contents

Introduction

Czesław Mesjasz, Katarzyna Bartusik, Tomasz Małkus, and Mariusz Sołtysik

Background

Since the 1980s such concepts as complexity, complex, emergence, chaos, the edge of chaos, non-linearity, self-organization, and related terms have become important components of management theory and practice. Similar phenomena can be observed in project management since the 1990s (Ireland and Statsenko 2020). Focusing on project management, including also software development, the following reasons for such a situation can be enumerated.

First, increasing uncertainty of the environment and increasing complexity of all kinds of projects, beginning from software development and ending with large-scale projects. This phenomenon must be seen in a broader context of globalization, the accelerated development of information technology, the increasing amount of produced and consumed information in society observed already in the 1980s, and the expansion of the Internet in the 1990s. The growing intricacy of organizations and the environment led to the development of management based on learning, intangible assets, networks, and processual orientation.

Second, these phenomena determined also the changes in software development and in project management. Traditional deterministic linear rigid methodologies were no longer adequate in dealing with new technologies, changing organizations and projects, and a rapidly evolving broadly defined environment. It could not leave unaffected all areas of project management and stimulated frequent references to intuitively interpretated complexity reflected in the large numbers of elements and their interactions, the differentiation of elements and interactions, and uncertainty concerning the environment, goals, and resources.

Third, in a parallel process, coinciding with the above phenomena, intuitive terms like complexity, uncertainty, and unpredictability, relevant to dynamically changing organizations, projects, and their environment, received in the 1990s additional interpretations from the development of the ideas collectively called complexity theory or complexity science which brought about such new ideas as complex adaptive systems, emerging properties, non-equilibrium, chaos illustrated with mathematical models, and metaphors.

DOI: 10.4324/9781003175032-1

In the 1990s, all those factors created a specific environment in which the notions complex, complexity, complex adaptive systems, chaos, edge of chaos, emergence, self-organization, and related terms had become the conceptual cornerstone of Scrum and adaptive software development (ASD) and exerted a significant direct and indirect impact on all other methodological frameworks collectively labelled Agile Project Management. In parallel, complexity-related ideas influenced also other domains of project management outside of the Agile software development methodological approaches.

It is definitely intellectually challenging to study the impact of complexity and variously defined complexity-related ideas on Agile Project Management. The number and variety of interpretations of complexity and of its characteristics are likely beyond any systematic studies.

At the same time, a deeper reflection on Agile also leads to paradoxical conclusions. How can we define or describe precisely something that by definition is elusive, volatile – just agile! The relations between the two concepts by themselves could be a fascinating object of theoretical considerations. Because the links between complexity and (in principle, not definable precisely), treated as a feature of organizations, and broadly defined projects play a rapidly growing role in the practice of modern management and of project management, the need for deepened studies seems essential.

This fundamental problem of modern project management requires a more detailed elucidation.

1. Changes in the environment of management and in project management
2. Necessity to adapt in software development
3. Complexity – coincidence with management and software development
4. Assessment of knowledge transfer
5. Identification and transfer of ideas

A broadly defined idea of Agile currently embodies a large number of applications, beginning from the initial classical domain – software development and project management at the small-scale level through multi-scale Agile Project Management and ending with Agile corporate management at all levels. We predominantly focus on the following areas of Agile Project Management (APM):

- Early ideas of APM developed in small-scale software development and project management
- Evolution and current state of small-scale Agile software development and project management
- Initial studies of the impact of complexity-related ideas on applications of Agile Project Management at the larger scale

Delineating the area of expansion of Agile-related ideas is currently impossible, but it is understandable that Agile Project Management at a large scale and Agile corporate management demand another study. In some cases we only signal the current and the forthcoming problems and solutions from these two areas.

Problem

Complexity-related concepts have been applied in management theory and practice as mathematical models, simulation models, analogies, and various figures of speech – predominantly metaphors. This phenomenon was carefully studied in the 1990s in management, and due to multiple uses and misuses, sometimes even as empty "buzzwords", the applications of complexity-related concepts gave rise to the dilemmas affecting all areas of management: "Fad or a promising concept" (McKelvey 1999) or "Fad or radical challenge" (Stacey *et al.* 2000) or perhaps, fashion (Price 2004)? In management theory and practice many concepts were regarded as fad. The basic question concerning fad is simple: Is it a concept, theory, method bringing about new ideas and solutions or is it just another temporal phenomenon or even fashion, with limited theoretical and practical value, which will sooner or later vanish and/or be undermined by critical studies (Newell *et al.* 2001)?

These questions were raised in the late 1990s and in the early 20th century after a dramatic increase in applications of complexity-related ideas in management theory and practice. From the current perspective, it is not possible to summarize the contribution of complexity-related ideas to management as a fad. The picture is more intricate. Yes, there were and there are numerous applications built on crude simplifications harmful to the theory and practice of management. However, in addition to insightful mathematical models and simulations, the studies of the complexity of organization based on analogies and metaphors taken from all complexity-related studies, including complexity science, delivered multiple new qualitative insights which were applicable as an instrument for enhancing creative thinking including predictions. They also stimulated new mathematical and simulation models. An open question remained to what extent the authors of such applications were/are aware of universal limitations of the applications of analogies and metaphors.

Similar questions remain behind our research, but our problem area is narrower. The majority of applications of complexity-related ideas in Agile methodological frameworks are based on analogies and metaphors. Additionally, since the onset of Agile in software development, references to complexity-related characteristics were regarded as its distinctive features.

Our main research question is thus as follows. How can we assess the significance of the multitude of complexity-related analogies and metaphors in the origins, development, and expansion of Agile methodological frameworks from software development to various areas of project management at different scales?

This fundamental and universal question can be decomposed into a set of more detailed questions concerning the transfer of ideas from complexity-oriented studies to Agile Project Management. What was the purpose and ontological, epistemological, and methodological value of such transfers? What could be the criteria of assessment of their usefulness? What were the advantages and weaknesses of those transfers of meaning from, say, complex adaptive systems in the development of Agile Project Management?

We do not go so far as to use the "fad-related" terminology in our study. Our approach is not strictly prescriptive. We just intend to show the evolution of applications of complexity-related ideas in the Agile Project Management area: The introduction of those ideas, expectations of them, their validity, the continuation of their applications, and their decreasing/increasing importance. The decisive factor for selecting such an approach is that the Agile methodological framework is not defined precisely. Struggling with the lack of precision in defining complexity and with the imprecision of defining Agile in project management would constitute an unachievable task.

From the wealth of problems and questions we have selected the essential ones. Assuming that a better understanding of the phenomena in one area can be helpful in another, thus it is necessary to study the relations between the source domain and target domain in the process of developing a metaphor. It is then necessary to investigate how the notions from one area can improve understanding in the second area.

Deeper studies of the multitude, variety, and scope of applications of complexity-related terms in APM allow us to conclude that in the simplest linguistic interpretation, they are used as metaphors. Rarely if ever, the uses of such terms are based upon more or less precise mathematical models capturing the complexity of the project team, the project environment, or the project itself. For example, it is not only the absence of mathematical models but the absence of any empirical evidence that allows the project team to be unequivocally depicted as being at the edge of chaos in the same way as the initial models of cellular automata for which that term was coined by Langton (1989, 1992) and made popular by Waldrop (1992, pp. 230–231).

The questions concerning the scientific value of the applications of all complexity-related ideas in APM derive from two fundamental theoretical and practical challenges. First, to what extent these ideas can be helpful in improving understanding of organizations and of their environment, and second, how this new knowledge can ameliorate management under those new circumstances. Answering these two questions is of a fundamental character in management and would require broader research.

This fundamental question leads to the problems of communication between different areas of knowledge and to the problems of interdisciplinarity. It translates into the need to assess the transfer of those new complexity-related ideas to management, and in our case, to project management. Putting all that in simpler language, we ask, if an observer looks at a project team as a self-organizing entity or treats innovations as emerging at the edge of chaos, to what extent does this understanding have new value for theory and practice? In other words, is this language more useful than the traditional language?

However, if we realize that the transfer of complexity-related ideas to management and to project management is accomplished predominantly with the use of metaphors, the problem becomes more intricate. We have to assess how the meaning of those concepts is created, their functions in project management, and the extent to which the results of this transfer can help in developing new theories and new applications.

The above remarks constitute a broader context of our research. The need for a more profound approach in studying the impact of a variety of complexity-related ideas on project management is mentioned in the following observation:

> We have almost reached the point where we rarely question what exactly we mean by these words [complex, complexity] or by the notion of "project complexity," and the more these phrases become part of the everyday project management language, the less attention is paid to what they stand for both theoretically and pragmatically.
>
> (Cicmil *at al.*, 2009)

The number of works responding directly and indirectly to the above reflection concerning the links between the various definitions of complexity and project management is quite large. They can be divided into the following groups:

1. Monographs referring to complexity and project management.
2. Overall syntheses of applications, predominantly journal articles, and websites of professional institutions specializing in training, consulting, and project implementation

Our research problem is narrower. Remembering the above reflection, we focus on the relations between broadly defined complexity-related ideas and Agile Project Management. A comprehensive survey of the existing body of knowledge reflected in the literature shows that there exists a significant research gap concerning theoretical and practical aspects of this problem.

Research questions

Due to the variety of interpretations of complexity – at least 45, according to (Lloyd 2001) – or even the impossibility of elaborating more specific definitions, attempts to give answers to those questions were made directly and indirectly in numerous earlier writings and recently published monographs on the applications of complexity and chaos-related ideas in management, e.g. (Allen *et al.* 2011; Jackson 2019). In project management broadly defined, similar appraisals of the applications of complexity-related terms were also made (Cicmil *et al.* 2009; Bakhshi *et al.* 2016).

Deeper studies of the multitude, variety, and scope of applications of complexity-related vocabulary in APM allow the conclusion that in the simplest linguistic interpretation, they are used as metaphors. Rarely the uses of such terms are based upon more or less precise mathematical models capturing the complexity of the project team, the project environment, or the project itself. For example, it is not only the impossibility to build mathematical models but also the lack of any empirical evidence that project team can be depicted as being at the edge of chaos in the same way as the initial models of cellular automata for which that term was coined by Langton (1989) and made popular by Waldrop (1992, pp.230–231).

The following research questions can be formulated:

1. Is the knowledge about various interpretations of complexity-related ideas sufficiently easily available for the theory and practice of project management and for Agile methodological frameworks in particular?
2. Which interpretations of complexity and complexity-related concepts have been applied in Agile Project Management and in project management broadly defined?
3. What was the impact of applications of complexity-related concepts on the origins and development of Agile Project Management?
4. What is the current status of applications of complexity-related ideas in APM?
5. How can those applications be assessed from the current perspective?
6. What could be the future directions of applications of complexity-related ideas in APM?

Aims

The main aim of this book is to identify the impact of applications of broadly defined complexity-related concepts on Agile Project Management since its onset until the beginning of the third decade of the 21st century.

The following partial aims are proposed:

1. Identification of interpretations of complexity and related concepts in project management broadly defined with the use of a new comprehensive typology of those interpretations.
2. Identification of the role of complexity-related ideas in the origins of APM.

3. Identification of the processes of creating and applying complexity-related metaphors in APM.
4. Ordering and preliminary assessment of the functions of applications of complexity-related ideas in APM.
5. A preliminary design of the processes of future applications of complexity-related concepts in Agile Project Management and in project management in general.

It is not our ambition to present a profound linguistic or hermeneutical analysis of the uses of complexity and related notions in Agile Project Management. We only would like to identify how those concepts were created and how they were transferred to the vocabulary and subsequently, to the theory and practice of APM. The proposed approach includes a preliminary analysis of the meaning of notions describing those concepts, e.g. complex, complexity, chaos, the edge of chaos, adaptation, which as metaphors have become dominating terms in all applications of the concept of Agile, not only in project management.

The study is based on the mixed research experience of our team. The long experience of Czesław Mesjasz in various areas of systems thinking, complexity studies, and in related areas, e.g. sociocybernetics, as well as in project management, is supplemented by the experience of the other members of the team in various areas of project management.

Conjectures

Having the results of that initial "archaeology of meaning" of these terms, we propose an initial conceptual framework for further theoretical studies of Agile Project Management necessary in dealing with complexity variously defined in the practice of project management.

Due to its scope, it is not possible to develop classically verifiable/falsifiable hypotheses in a broad survey-like study. Bearing in mind the above assumptions, the following conjectures are scrutinized:

1. The terms complexity, chaos, the edge of chaos, and related terms played a decisive role in the development of project management methodological approaches initially applied in Agile.
2. In spite of declarations of the links between the APM and mathematical models labelled as complexity theory (chaos theory), no direct links between the models and project management – including Scrum and other APM methodological frameworks – can be identified. Only more or less vaguely defined metaphors are applied.
3. Complexity-related terms applied in APM fulfil a broad variety of functions of metaphors: Linguistic, cognitive, and communicative. In some cases they can be treated as persuasive and sometimes even performative utterances.

4. Applications of the complexity-related terms in project management have to be assessed with the use of knowledge from complexity studies, linguistics, psychology, cognitive science, and deepened knowledge about the specificity of advanced projects. This initial appraisal should help in elaborating more effective interdisciplinary approaches in managing various types of projects, not only in software development under the conditions of complexity, self-organization, and limited predictability of the final results.

In a preliminary survey of interpretations of complexity-related terms and the elaboration of a new framework approach, a simple analysis of the texts is sufficient. The results of our research constitute a point of departure for further deepened studies with applications of more advanced methods of data-mining and text-mining. As is always the case with literature-based studies, a necessarily harsh selection from a large collection of surveyed works and documents had to be performed.

An important factor determining all discussions on the practice and theory of Agile Project Management must be taken into account. The proponents of making project management flexible, adaptable, etc., always face the fundamental paradox: How to define something more precisely that by definition is agile – imprecise, capturing uncertainty, unpredictability, adaptation, and learning.

Methods

Complexity, complex, emergence, chaos, edge of chaos, equilibrium, non-linearity, self-organization, and other terms have become a part of project management vocabulary since the 1990s. For the sake of simplification we propose to call them complexity-related notions. A closer look at the occurrences of those notions, in project management, similarly as in management, allows us to disclose an interesting phenomenon.

Usually applications of complexity-related ideas in project management, similarly as in management, are associated with complexity science which, preliminarily, can be described as a family of mathematical models associated with such concepts as complex adaptive systems, emergence, self-organization, chaos, the edge of chaos, and many others. These mathematical models are also the source domains for analogies and metaphors in management and in project management.

We should also remember other applications of complexity and associated terms in management and in project management, which have been borrowed from cybernetics and systems thinking. In addition, and it is especially visible in project management, intuitive interpretations of complexity are still used. As an example, the works can be recalled which have complexity in the title but no direct references to complexity science can be found.

So as to avoid any terminological misunderstandings, in the next part of this book the interpretations of complexity science, cybernetics, systems thinking, and their mutual relations will be explained in detail.

Audience

Due to the popularity of applications of complexity-related ideas in project management including Agile Project Management, since its very onset our project has been designed as addressed to a broader audience. We expect that it will be useful for all practitioners of project management who are confronted with various, more or less detailed interpretations of complexity of projects and their environment in the applications of Agile Project Management. It can be treated as an introductory guidebook describing the past role of complexity-related ideas not only in Agile Project Management.

It may be also expected that a study of the meanings and applications of complexity and related ideas in APM and in project management in general will be helpful for researchers and for the institutions engaged in developing standards of project management. Additionally, although the book is focused on Agile and project management, it may be anticipated that our book may be also a source of inspiration in the process of the expansion of Agile beyond project management.

It must be emphasized that the book includes the preliminary results of our research. Therefore, many ideas are presented here in an introductory way. We are perfectly aware that multiple issues have to be discussed and studied more profoundly. It concerns the weaknesses of the book for which we feel fully accountable. Our project has not been finished yet and we hope that our future research will allow to improve the weaknesses and to show and assess new possibilities of applications of complexity-related ideas in Agile Project Management.

We would like to express our gratitude to the entire editorial team of Routledge, Taylor & Francis Group who helped us in publishing this book.

The monograph was created as part of a project financed by the Minister of Education and Science within the "Regional Initiative of Excellence" Programme for 2019–2022. Project no.: 021/RID/2018/19. Total financing: 11,897,131.40 PLN.

References

Allen, P., Maguire, S. and McKelvey, B. (eds) (2011) *The Sage handbook of complexity and management.* Los Angeles, CA: SAGE.

Bakhshi, J., Ireland, V. and Gorod, A. (2016) Clarifying the project complexity construct: Past, present and future. *International Journal of Project Management,* Vol. 34, No. 7, pp. 1199–1213. doi: 10.1016/j.ijproman.2016.06.002.

Cicmil, S., Cooke-Davies, T., Crawford, L. and Richardson, K. (2009) *Exploring the complexity of projects: Implications of complexity theory for project management practice.* Newtown Square, PA: PMI (Kindle edition).

Ireland, V. and Statsenko, L. (2020) Managing complex projects and systems: A literature synthesis. *Australian Journal of Multi-Disciplinary Engineering,* Vol. 16, No. 1, pp. 93–110. doi: 10.1080/14488388.2020.1805861.

Jackson, M.C. (2019) *Critical systems thinking and the management of complexity. Responsible leadership for a complex world.* Hoboken, NJ: John Wiley & Sons.

Langton, C. G. (1989) Artificial Life, in: C. G. Langton (ed), *Artificial Life: The Proceedings of an Interdisciplinary Workshop on the Synthesis and Simulation of Living Systems. SFI Studies in the Sciences of Complexity, Proceedings, Vol. 6.* Redwood City, CA: Addison-Wesley, pp. 1–48.

Langton, C. G.(1992). Life at the edge of chaos in: C. G. Langton, C. Taylor, J.D. Farmer and S. Rasmussen (eds), *Artificial Life II. Santa Fe Institute Studies in the Sciences of Complexity, Proceedings, vol. 10 (Proceedings of second Artificial Life workshop, 1990).* Redwood City, CA: Addison-Wesley, pp. 41–91.

Lloyd, S. (2001) Measures of complexity: A nonexhaustive list. *IEEE Control Systems Magazine*, Vol. 21, No. 4, pp. 7–8. doi: 10.1109/MCS.2001.939938.

McKelvey, B. (1999) Complexity theory in organization science: Seizing the promise or becoming a fad? *Emergence*, Vol. 1, No. 1, pp. 5–32. doi: 10.1207/S15327000EM0101_2.

Newell, S., Robertson, M. and Swan, J. (2001) Management fads and fashions. *Organization*, Vol. 8, No. 1, pp. 5–15. doi: 10.1177/135050840181001.

Price, I. (2004) Complexity, complicatedness and complexity: A new science behind organizational intervention? *E:CO*, Vol. 6, No. 1–2, pp. 40–48.

Stacey, R.D., Griffin, D. and Shaw, P. (2000) *Complexity and management. Fad or radical challenge to systems thinking.* London and New York: Routledge.

Waldrop, M.M. (1992) *Complexity: The emerging science at the edge of order and chaos.* New York: Simon & Schuster.

1 Conceptual framework

Assumptions of the study

Detailed descriptions of assumptions, explanations, and definitions may sometimes seem excessive and unneeded. In this book it is not incidental. There are two reasons for such an approach. First, because the majority of applications of complexity-related ideas are metaphors and other linguistic constructs (similes, metonymies), therefore we purposively conduct a kind of "archaeology of knowledge" trying to show the journey of some notions from the source domain of analogies and metaphors to their target domains. In consequence, it gives the reader a chance to better learn the meanings of the terms applied in the theory and practice of project management and of Agile in particular. Second, since it is commonly agreed that more complex projects will be developed with APM, therefore the level of knowledge about complexity among theoreticians and practitioners in Agile should be ameliorated. Too often, the consequences of complexity for Agile are presented with superficial descriptions.

Complexity and management, project management, and Agile Project Management

When studying the role of complexity in Agile Project Management we have to remember that it should always be seen in the context of a three-level hierarchy of containment of complexity-related ideas. The first-level ideas were developed in such domains as cybernetics, systems thinking, system dynamics, systems engineering, and complexity science. This level includes the fundamental initial concepts – abstract mathematical models and their applications in modelling collective phenomena in physics, chemistry, biology, engineering, and variously defined socioeconomic systems. The second level embodies the applications of complexity-related ideas in management. Project management broadly defined, including Agile Project Management, which, in turn, includes software projects and other types of projects, can be treated as the third level.

A question arises: What are the relations between levels two and three? Evidently the third level is included in the second one. It will have to be

DOI: 10.4324/9781003175032-2

recalled sometimes since not always all applications of complexity-related concepts used in management are relevant to project management. Distinctive features of management and project management include the temporary character of projects, the specificity of risk management, and the specificity of stakeholders relation.

The Agile Project Management frameworks constitute the most specific field where complexity and associated ideas have become equally important as in management. According to the propositions in the fundamental works, it embodies applications of non-software Agile Project Management frameworks and Agile software development – see Figure 1.1.

The distinction between project management and management is necessary since they are not identical and the former is a part of the latter. Usually in the literature on applications of complexity-related ideas in project management this distinction is omitted. In our study we keep in mind this phenomenon, and whenever necessary we expose the specificity of complexity in project management broadly defined in relation to complexity in management.

The difference between project management and management understood in a broader sense must be taken into account. It is of special importance in our study. Of course, a project is a special, temporarily limited type of organization. In the theory of project management, the following approaches can be found. First, no distinctions are made as to expose specificity of both areas, and the fundamental characteristics such as, for example, strategy and relations with stakeholders are treated as similar. Second, it is assumed that project management constitutes a specific, well-defined part of management understood in a

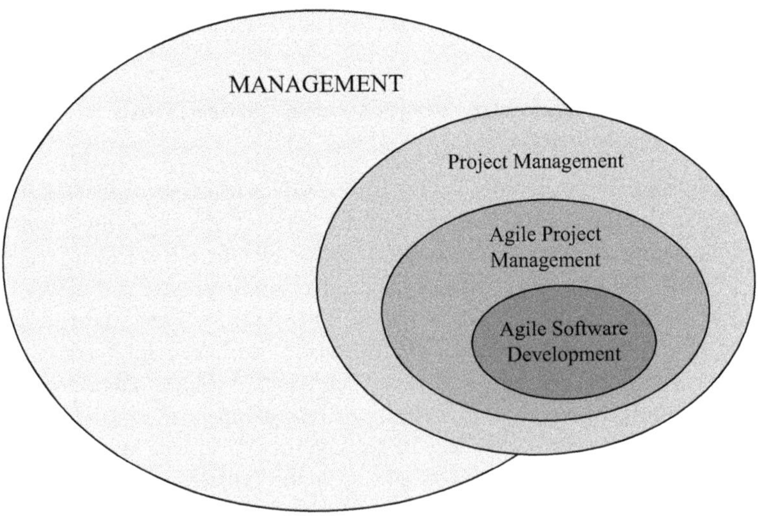

Figure 1.1 Relations between management, project management, and Agile Project Management. Source: Own research.

broader sense. In our study the main area of applications of complexity-related concepts is project management. Whenever necessary, we expose the distinctive facets of management and of project management.

Terminology

Terminological precision constitutes one of most important challenges in inter- and multi-disciplinary studies. Our approach towards the terminology is as follows. We realize how many different definitions and interpretations of various terms can be found in the research area encapsulating complexity-related ideas and Agile Project Management. At the same time it is also well-known that precise definition is neither possible nor necessary. However a certain compromise must always be found especially for the facilitation of communication in academic discourse and between theory and practice. Additionally, the care for reasonable precision of interpretations is necessary in the era of constructivism and interpretative approaches in management theory. The meaning can be created in the discourse, but some initial interpretations always have to be presented. It is of special importance when the idea of Agile in project management defined in multiple ways is confronted with also not too-precisely defined ideas associated with complexity.

The first terminological problem derives from the meaning of the term agile. Etymology and definitions of this term are explained later. Here it is only necessary to explain when the term is used as an adjective and noun and when it is used as a proper name. In all situations when a new approach in project management is associated with the methodological frameworks declared by their authors as agile in the Agile Manifesto (2001) then the uppercase first letter is used. Uppercase characters are also used in Agile Project Management. Elsewhere lowercase characters begin the term agile. The same rule concerns the term agility.

Further explanation is needed for the terms organizational theory (theory of organization), management theory, and organization and management theory (as the name of a Division of the Academy of Management). In the majority of texts in management they are either used interchangeably or without any deepened reflection. So as to avoid any doubts and long discussions we use the terms theory of organization and management theory interchangeably with full awareness of terminological doubts and discussions.

Agile and project management: Method, practice, methodology, or approach

Other definitional doubts are associated with the variety of interpretations of the term Agile in relation to project management. This problem will be discussed in detail in the remainder of the book. In this introductory part it is only necessary to explain the meaning of Agile as a methodological concept and/or a methodological framework. For the sake of brevity, wherever in the text the term Agile is standing alone it can be interpretated as Agile Project Management defined in the first chapter and relating to software development and project management. It is always properly indicated when the term Agile is used in reference to various areas of corporate management.

One of the consequences of complexity narratives for complexity is the multitude of more or less precise and formally logically correct definitions, or rather interpretations, of complexity, chaos, and akin terms in science and in practice. So as to avoid extensive definitional considerations, we propose using the term interpretations in reference to all attempts to define more or less precisely that notion. This approach is not a novelty since in multiple works dealing with complexity, broadly defined, and its characteristics, the authors often do not formulate definitions fulfilling the demands of classical logical correctness and leave the readers with more or less confusing interpretations.

We propose to use the following terminology. In addition to using the terms complex and complexity we apply the notions of complexity-related ideas, concepts, terms, etc. These notions embody not only the words complex and complexity but also the characteristics usually associated with various interpretations of complexity. As an example, chaos theory can be used. As it will be shown later, in some sources, the terms chaos theory and complexity theory are applied separately, while in other cases, they are put under the umbrella of complexity science and/or complexity theory.

The literature on complexity is teeming with ideas, definitions, and interpretations. As a natural consequence, we quote only a fraction of the sources, although we tried to collect the most representative ones. It can be easily spotted that reference to the fundamental works on complexity-related ideas is not incidental. Without mentioning specific sources, it can be observed that a large number of works applying the ideas relating to complexity are superficial and not always useful for theoreticians and practitioners.

Agile Project Management: Origins and status quo. Beginnings of the Agile approach in software development

A survey of literature in management, software development, and project management allows for the conclusion that the idea of Agile has passed through a specific, in some sense, a cyclical evolution. From production management and management, through software development and project management to multiple areas of industry, the economy, and society – manufacturing, trade, health service, education, etc. The term Agile is even viewed as a new paradigm in project management and in management. In some cases, claims are made that all areas of human activity should be "Agile". Such an expansion may lead to justifiable criticisms. If something has too broad a scope of meaning it could be useless from a logical and cognitive point of view.

In dealing with Agile and complexity, two concepts which both have multiple and fuzzy interpretations, it is necessary to clarify their meaning to the degree which would allow a sufficient level of communication. Explanations of the interpretations of complexity will come later; now we focus on the notion agile. Etymology and dictionaries help as an introduction to more advanced studies. Etymologically the term agile, meaning having quickness of motion, nimble, active (of body or mind) derives from the French agile and directly from the Latin *agilis*, "nimble, quick" (Online Etymology Dictionary). Merriam-Webster Dictionary defines agile as: 1: Marked by ready ability to move with quick easy grace an agile dancer; 2: having a quick resourceful and adaptable character and agile mind.

Studying the impact of complexity-related concepts on the origins and development of Agile Project Management requires giving at least preliminary answers to the following questions:

1) What were the origins of assigning the term agile to various methodological concepts in management, software development, and project management?
2) What concepts are assigned to the group of Agile methodological frameworks in software development and in project management?
3) What were the directions of evolution of Agile methodological frameworks in software development and in project management?

References

Principles behind the Agile Manifesto (2001) http://agilemanifesto.org/principles.html
Merriam-Webster Dictionary (2019) https://www.merriam-webster.com/dictionary/.
Online Etymology Dictionary, https://www.etymonline.com.

2 Theoretical background and methods of research

Complexity-related models, analogies, and metaphors in Agile Project Management

The definitions and interpretations of complexity as well as the definitions and interpretations of Agile stir fundamental ontological, epistemological, and methodological questions. In the ontological discussions about complexity, the main challenge is whether there is something like objectively existing "complexity" (parentheses are not incidental) or whether complexity is a social construct deriving from the relations between observer and observed object. This problem would require additional reflection; therefore it is only assumed that in studying the influence of complexity-related ideas on Agile Project Management an interpretative approach and cognitive approaches are applied – complexity is a feature of the relations between observer and observed objects. In the most fundamental sense, it was stressed by Gell-Mann that even the complexity of physical, chemical, and biological systems has its roots in relations between observer and observed object (Gell-Mann 1994, p. 33). It will be given more attention when the role of the observer in studying complexity is analysed in the remainder of the book.

In management, and subsequently in Agile Project Management, the key questions are the characteristics of the system (organization). Is the organization like a natural or engineering system which can be more or less precisely studied as an objective, independent from the observer, or is it just a social construct created in an intersubjective process? It can be concluded that both options are legitimate. If an organization is more or less precisely depicted with measurable parameters and then studied with mathematical models/simulation models then we may apply approaches taken from physics, biology, and engineering ("hard" systems thinking and "hard" complexity). However, when such an approach is not achievable, then the situation becomes more intricate. We deal with "soft" complexity depicted with qualitative narratives or mixed, qualitative/quantitative narratives. It has to be remembered that in both approaches, "hard" and mixed, mathematics is treated as just a language and not as the essence of being. This explanation requires further philosophical elucidation.

DOI: 10.4324/9781003175032-3

The questions arising from this dilemma have been, at least partly, answered by Ralph Stacey, one of the most influential authors in the field of applications of complexity-related ideas in management. While in his early studies, he assumed, not always explicitly, that organization as defined in management is a system in the engineering sense, in his later works, he admitted that organization may not be treated as such a system and it is a product of human interactions described in the complex responsive processes of relating (CRPR). This idea has been presented in several works of Stacey and his co-workers. It is described here in an introductory way with reference to (Stacey 2000; Stacey *et al.* 2000).

Following this assumption, we treat all complexity-related concepts applied in project management as analogies and metaphors. It is a simplifying assumption, but it leads to a very insightful approach in studying the relations between variously defined complexity-related characteristics of projects, organizations, project teams, environment, and Agile Project Management in particular.

This assumption demands a broader explanation. In the most general sense, complexity-related concepts are used in the theory and practice of project management such as mathematical models, simulation models, analogies, and various types of figures of speech – metaphors, similes, and metonyms.

Looking at the wealth of discussions in that area, it may be concluded that metaphors are a dominant form of application of complexity-related ideas in Agile Project Management, and they are more frequent than in project management and in management. This phenomenon derives from the very broad interpretation of Agile. We do not neglect other figures of speech but for the sake of simplicity, following an example of Holland (1998, p. 207), not undermining the exactness of our study, we concentrate our attention on analogies and metaphors remembering that in more detailed studies similes, metonyms, and other tropes have also to be taken into account.

The use of analogies and metaphors taken from physics, chemistry, biology, and engineering in studying social systems creates a very specific demand. In all cases the authors using those metaphors should be aware of the transfer of the meaning from the source domain to the target domain. Unfortunately, these metaphors are often misunderstood, simplified, and misused, Two extreme situations can be quoted. The metaphors are either treated as "scientific" without deeper reflection by specialists from outside social sciences, or on the contrary, are used as void slogans by theoreticians and practitioners from management.

The assumption of the decisive role of analogies and metaphors in transferring knowledge about various characteristics of complexity to Agile Project Management also derives from a more balanced assessment which can be made thanks to the current time perspective. At present, now that the initial fascination has disappeared, we better know the advantages and disadvantages of applications of complexity-related ideas in social sciences.

Looking at a variety of soft interpretations of complexity, it may be argued that the specific concepts taken from such areas as cybernetics and broadly defined systems thinking, when applied in studying social systems, were accepted as metaphors, e.g. the self-fulfilling prophecy as an example of positive feedback.

The main source of doubts concerning the metaphorical interpretations of complexity and its characteristics concerns the applications of the ideas taken from complexity science. The role of metaphors was already seen in the early period of development of complexity science in the title of one of the first books summarizing the results of the first conferences held at the Santa Fe Institute (Cowan *et al.* 1994).

Morgan (1986, 2006; Cornelissen *et al.* 2008) and many other authors laid the ground for more profound discussions on the role of metaphors in management. Being aware of a wealth of literature on analogies, metaphors, and other linguistic constructs, due to practical reasons, we refer to a limited number of sources. First and foremost, it is necessary to recall basic definitions of analogy, metaphor, and linguistics concepts associated with the latter. Metaphor is a figure of speech in which a word or phrase literally denoting one kind of object or idea is used in place of another to suggest a likeness or analogy between them (Merriam-Webster Dictionary 2019). According to the same source, analogy is "comparison of two otherwise unlike things based on resemblance of a particular aspect".

There are multiple definitions and typologies of metaphors and of related concepts. The following distinctions between metaphor, simile, and metonymy deriving from the Merriam-Webster Online Dictionary seem to be sufficient in this introductory study. Whenever necessary they can be scrutinized in depth with other sources. Simile differs from metaphor by the use of the notions as or like. Metonymy is a figure of speech consisting of the use of the name of one thing for that of another of which it is an attribute or with which it is associated (such as "crown" in "lands belonging to the crown").

The basic cognitive structure of analogy, metaphor, and associated terms consists of the source domain and the target domain. Different patterns of projection of the meaning of the notions in both domains determine typological differences – see Figure 2.1.

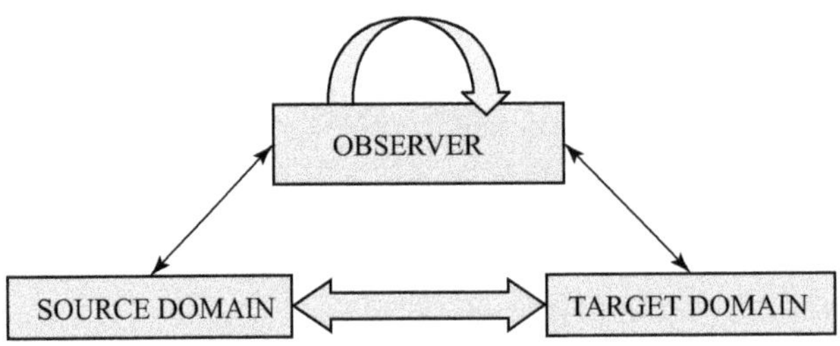

Figure 2.1 Relations between the source domain and target domain in analogies and metaphors with taking into account self-reflexivity. Source: Own research.

In Figure 2.1 a specific element is added showing that the application of metaphor includes also a self-reflection of the observer. It is of special importance when the role of the observer in building metaphors is included in studying complexity and metaphors.

Leaving aside variety, differences, and critics as well as advantages and disadvantages of definitions of metaphor studies in works by Lakoff and Johnson (1980/1993), Lakoff (1993), Steen (2007, 2008, 2017), and Steen *et al.* (2010), in this preliminary study the following types of metaphors are referred to: Conceptual metaphors, deliberate metaphors, live metaphors, and dead metaphors.

Lakoff and Johnson (1980) have introduced the conceptual metaphor in which knowledge about the source domain allows for understanding the target domain. Conceptual metaphor is not only a linguistic tool but an instrument for shaping human thinking and human actions.

According to Steen (2017, pp. 1–2), deliberate metaphor derives from its intentional use between sender and addressee. This definition minimally implies that language users, in production or reception, pay distinct attention to the source domain as a separate domain of reference.

In the simplest sense, live metaphor reflects a property of an object which is new for it and allows for discovering its new features like for example the concept of Morgan (1986, 2006) – organization as machine, organization as a living system, etc. "Dead" metaphors on the other hand have evolved further into a situation where the metaphorical meaning has become the meaning for a word or an alternative meaning for a word (polysemy). In the most universal sense, the divide between live metaphor and dead metaphor is treated as a simplification (Lakoff and Johnson 1980/1995; Cornelissen *et al.* 2008).

The primary function of metaphor is to provide a partial understanding of one kind of experience in terms of another kind of experience. This may involve preexisting isolated similarities, the creation of new similarities, and more. More specifically, metaphors have linguistic, cognitive, and communicative functions. They also may be divertive in literature and conversation, informative in news and science, persuasive in advertising, politics, and science, and instructive in education. Thus, metaphor may be regarded as an essential tool in language, thought, and communication (Steen 2008, pp. 213–214). Metaphors viewed as elements of the vocabulary of theory can be applied for description, explanation of causal relations, prediction, anticipation, and prescriptive recommendations. They concern both a positivist/neopositivist approach, and an interpretative and post-modernist approach.

Metaphors may have a significant heuristic value as expressing something that could not be expressed otherwise but is not yet operational. They also stimulate learning and innovativeness. Mathematical models, analogies, and metaphors deriving from complexity science are gaining a special significance in management and in project management. They are treated as "scientific" and obtain supplementary intellectual (and persuasive) influence resulting from "sound" normative (precisely prescriptive) legitimacy in management, and subsequently, in project management.

Because the complexity-related metaphors have an additional scientific character in project management described above, thus their persuasive functions also will be preliminarily studied (Sopory and Dillard 2002). Finally, in Agile Project Management treated as an applied and normative area of knowledge and practice, some metaphorical utterances may also become performative utterances (acts of speech) (Austin 1962; Searle 1995; Tseng and Lin 2011).

The questions concerning applications of complexity-related ideas as metaphors in Agile Project Management (APM) are as follows: (1) How have the metaphors based on various "hard" complexity-related concepts been interpreted in the development of APM? (2) What are the functions of those metaphors? (3) To what extent should theoreticians and practitioners engaged in creating and applying those metaphors in Agile Project Management be aware of the transfer of meaning from the "source domains" to the "target domains"?

Methods and sources

In the studies of applications of complexity-related concepts in Agile Project Management methodological approaches, the following issues were taken into account:

1) Identification of occurrence – which component of Agile Project Management (project, project team, organizations – project developer and customer, stakeholders, environment) was associated with complexity-related ideas.
2) Interpretations of the relations of complexity-related notions with APM.
3) Sources of the complexity-related concepts – references to literature.
4) Pattern of relations between source field and target field when the concept is treated as analogy and/or metaphoric.
5) Assessment of the relevance of the complexity-related concept to the attributes of APM.
6) Evolution of the impact of complexity-related ideas on specific concepts taken from Agile Project Management.

The proposed study is designed as an introduction to further investigations embodying more profound and extensive text mining analysis and a deepened understanding. Usually in text mining research the terms used in the texts under study should be relatively precisely defined. Unfortunately, the notions complexity and Agile have numerous interpretations, and thus trying just to count the frequency of their occurrence and identify their meaning – direct and context-determined – would only show how often the observers apply those terms with a limited possibility of more advanced interpretations. In the case of complexity, such an approach would be reduced to only an initial study showing which notions are most frequently perceived as synonymous with complex and complexity. Due to a broad meaning of the term Agile the results would be similar.

We have two parallel aims in studying complexity-related ideas as metaphors applied in Agile Project Management. The first, theoretical, is to develop a point of departure for more profound studies pointing out specific interpretations of the notions associated with complexity and Agile Project Management. The terminological considerations are treated as a starting platform and a guide for further, more methodologically advanced studies. The second aim is practical, to provide theoreticians and practitioners with a more profound and comprehensive understanding of relations between complexity-related ideas and the practice of APM and of their consequences. The above factors concerning the scope of meaning of complexity-related terms and Agile Project Management determine the methods of our detailed studies of the content of the texts.

Agile Project Management derives from earlier concepts of software development and project management. They constituted a context for the creation of APM. Therefore we study not only the applications of complexity-related ideas in Agile Project Management. A broad variety of works linking project management in a universal sense and complexity-related ideas are included in our study. However, deepened studies of metaphors deriving from complexity studies are predominantly focused on Agile Project Management.

Because of its introductory character, this study is built on a classical literature survey performed with detailed studies of the texts of publications and browsing of the databases.

There is one specific facet of our research. In addition to classical sources – books and journals (printed and websites), databases of journals and publishing companies, and comprehensive databases like Scopus, World of Science, and Mendeley – we had to make a selection from the sources available on the Internet. In this case we had to consider a specific hurdle of the search. There are likely scores of websites of large and small consulting companies, websites, and blogs of individuals and discussion groups more or less closely associated with Agile Project Management. Some of them provide new insights – theoretical and practice-oriented. Some of them are long-lasting, and some are just ephemeral. For the sake of simplicity and as to avoid significant misunderstandings deriving from not always well-documented sources of information on multiple websites, the scope and number of Internet sources are limited. Otherwise it would be necessary to maintain additional assessment and selection of those sources.

Being familiar with a large number of works in which complexity-related ideas are applied as metaphors in Agile Project Management, we had to choose a relevant method of studying those works. As the source of methodological inspiration we have used the Metaphor Identification Procedure Vrije

Universiteit (MIPVU) developed by Steen and co-researchers (Steen *et al.* 2010). We treat this methodology as a conceptual framework, and its application depends on the type and circumstances of the use of metaphors described in each relevant chapter.

An extended bibliography of all types of sources is also a part of the results of our research. It can be frequently observed that in the studies of applications of complexity-related ideas in management, the authors do not always perform sufficiently precise "archaeology of knowledge" and use secondary or even tertiary sources, very often distorting the initial concepts. It is of special importance in the studies of analogies and metaphors. In the case of complexity-related ideas and Agile Project Management, a carefully selected list of the most significant sources can be helpful in developing further studies not only in Agile Project Management but also in other applications of the concept of Agile.

References

Austin, J.L. (1962) *How to do things with words.* Oxford: Clarendon.

Cornelissen, J.P., Oswick, C., Christensen, L.T. and Phillips, N. (2008) Metaphor in organizational research: Context, modalities and implications for research. *Organization Science*, Vol. 29, No. 1, pp. 7–22. doi: 10.1177/0170840607086634.

Cowan, G., Pines, D. and Meltzer, D. (eds) (1994) *Complexity: Metaphors, models, and reality. Santa Fe Institute. Studies in the Sciences of Complexity, Proceedings.* Reading, MA: Addison-Wesley

Gell-Mann, M. (1994) *The quark and the jaguar: Adventures in the simple and the complex.* New York: W.H. Freeman and Company.

Holland, J.D. (1998) *Emergence: From chaos to order.* Reading, MA: Addison-Wesley.

Lakoff, G. (1993) The contemporary theory of metaphor. In A. Ortony (ed.), *Metaphor and thought*, 2nd edition. Cambridge: Cambridge University Press, pp. 202–251.

Lakoff, G. and Johnson, M. (1980/1995) *Metaphors we live by.* Chicago, IL: University of Chicago Press.

Merriam-Webster Dictionary (2019) https://www.merriam-webster.com/dictionary/.

Morgan, G. (1986) *Images of organization.* London: SAGE.

Morgan, G. (2006) *Images of organization*, 2nd edition. Thousand Oaks, CA: SAGE.

Newell, S., Robertson, M. and Swan, J. (2001) Management fads and fashions. *Organization*, Vol. 8, No. 1, pp. 5–15. doi: 10.1177/135050840181001.

Searle, J. R. (1995) *The construction of social reality.* New York: The Free Press.

Sopory, P. and Dillard, J.P. (2002) Figurative comparison and persuasion. In J.P. Dillard and M. W. Pfau (eds), *The persuasion handbook: Developments in theory and practice.* Thousand Oaks, CA: Sage.

Stacey, R.D. (2000) *Strategic management & organizational dynamics*, 3rd edition. The Challenge of Complexity. Harlow: Pearson Education Limited.

Stacey, R.D., Griffin, D. and Shaw, P. (2000) *Complexity and management. Fad or radical challenge to systems thinking.* London and New York: Routledge.

Steen, G.J. (2007) *Finding metaphor in grammar and usage: A methodological analysis of theory and research.* Amsterdam and Philadelphia: John Benjamins.

Steen, G. (2008) The paradox of metaphor: Why we need a three-dimensional model of metaphor. *Metaphor and Symbol*, Vol. 23, No. 4, pp. 213–241.

Steen, G. (2017) Deliberate metaphor theory: Basic assumptions, main tenets, urgent issues. *Intercultural Pragmatics*, Vol. 14, No. 1, pp. 1–24.

Steen, G. J., Dorst, A. G., Herrmann, J. B., Kaal, A. A., Krennmayr, T., and Pasma, T. (2010) *A method for linguistic metaphor identification. From MIP to MIPVU. (Converging Evidence in Language and Communication Research; No. 14)*. Amsterdam: John Benjamins.

Tseng, Y.-H. and Lin, C.-T. (2011) Enhancing enterprise agility by deploying agile drivers, capabilities and providers. *Information Sciences*, Vol. 181, No. 17, pp. 3693–3708.

3 Typology of interpretations of complexity-related concepts in Agile Project Management

Complex and complicated: Introductory interpretations

Scores of works on complexity begin with the famous quote of Stephen Hawking from an interview with the *San Jose Mercury News* in 2000 (Chui 2000): "The twenty-first century will be the century of complexity". While a universal sense of this statement remains valid, the 20-year time perspective allows for a more deepened reflection on the undefined complexity which is supposed to affect our lives.

Definitional, terminological, and typological problems constitute a significant part of discussions on cybernetics, sociocybernetics, systems thinking, and the areas of research called complexity theory, complexity theories complexity science. The interpretations of complexity terms are especially difficult since this notion has multiple interpretations, beginning from intuitive, common-sense ideas, through cybernetics, systems thinking, complexity science, advanced studies touching the foundations of mathematics, and ending with various qualitative interpretations.

In discussing the interpretations of complexity we face the dilemma. On the one hand we know that it is not possible to define complexity unequivocally. On the other, we have to remember the statement made by Holland (2006, p. 6): "It is not likely that precise definitions of 'complexity', 'emergence', or the like, are necessary for studies of complex systems to proceed rapidly". However, in studying social systems we have to use a more precise meaning so as to make sense of complexity and to communicate efficiently.

Before presenting a typology of interpretations of complexity in project management, a brief reflection on the meaning of complex, complicated, and simple is needed. In the studies of complexity of any object three general approaches can be defined – intuitive, mathematical, and attempts to develop more precise qualitative interpretations. Combinations of all three non-ideal types are common.

In most general sense, intuitive terms complex/complexity uttered by an observer reflect a large number of elements, their interactions, variety of interactions, variability, unpredictability, uncertainty, emerging properties, impossibility to decompose a system into elements, etc. Leaving apart the discussion

DOI: 10.4324/9781003175032-4

about universal definitions of system and its complexity, the following intuitive and more rigorously defined characteristics of complexity of social system, inspired, but not only, by (Gell-Mann 1984; Cilliers 1998; Allen *et al.* 2011; Stacey and Mowles 2016) can be quoted.

1) Large number of interacting elements (physical interactions and/or informational interactions).
2) Dominance of short-range interactions with possibility of impact of long-range interactions.
3) Non-linear interactions with feedback and recurrence.
4) Open systems, often with fuzzily defined borders.
5) Path-dependence ("history matters").
6) System in a far-from-equilibrium state.
7) Limited information of element about the state of system – from the lack of information (biological systems) to partial information – human systems – holons (Koestler 1967).
8) Hierarchical structure (various types of hierarchy – functional, subordination, containment, nested).

The meaning of the terms complex and complicated requires additional elucidation of its differences with also the intuitive and analytical sense of complicated. There are several interpretations of complicated systems. A convincing interpretation was proposed by Cilliers (1998, p. xiii–ix). If a system composed of a large number of components can be given a complete description in terms of its individual constituents, such a system is merely complicated, e.g. jumbo jets or computers. In a complex system, the interaction among constituents of the system, and the interaction between the system and its environment, are of such a nature that the system as a whole cannot be fully understood simply by analysing its components. Moreover, these relationships are not fixed and could be the results of emergence and of self-organization. In the Cynefin framework complicated is associated with known unknown and knowable unknown characteristics of a system and its environment (Kurtz and Snowden 2003; Snowden and Goh 2021).

Complex, complexity, and complicated should be always studied in reference to the simple. This problem, especially important for complexity science and in applications in management and in project management, is discussed in detail in the parts devoted to detailed interpretations of complexity.

Assumptions of typology

Definitional, terminological, and typological problems constitute a significant part of discussions on cybernetics, sociocybernetics, systems thinking, and the areas called complexity theory or complexity science. The interpretations of complexity and of complexity-related terms are especially difficult since this notion has multiple interpretations, beginning from intuitive, common-sense ideas, through cybernetics, systems thinking, complexity science, advanced studies touching the foundations of mathematics.

Does this mean that we have to resign from a better understanding of the multitude of interpretations of complexity and related concepts? Of course not, but caution and depth of study are necessary.

There were multiple attempts to develop and to systematize definitions and interpretations of complexity and its related terms: 45 interpretations of complexity by Lloyd (2001), comprehensive synthetizing works (anything earlier Prigogine and Stengers 1984; Waldrop 1992; Casti 1994; Bar-Yam 1997; Biggiero 2001; Gleick 1987/2008; Warfield 2006; Castellani and Hafferty 2009; Castellani and Gerrits 2021). As a special contribution the monumental *Encyclopedia of Complexity and Systems Science* (2009) must be added to this collection. Similar efforts have been made in management literature (Stacey 1996; Brown and Eisenhardt 1998; Anderson 1999; Stacey *et al.* 2000; Moldoveanu 2004; Allen *et al.* 2011; Boulton *et al.* 2015; Stacey and Mowles 2016; Jackson 2019).

Since the 1980s, studies of the role of complexity in project management in a universal sense began to appear. It is impossible to quote all of them so only selected influential works are recalled: (Baccarini 1996; Williams 1999, 2002; Cooke-Davies *et al.* 2007; Cicmil *et al.* 2009; Whitty and Maylor 2009; Geraldi *et al.* 2011; *Navigating Complexity* 2014; Ahern *et al.* 2014; Botchkarev and Finnigan 2015; Bakhshi *et al.* 2016; Poveda-Bautista *et al.* 2018; Ireland and Statsenko 2020; Mikkelsen 2020). Parallelly, the role of complexity in project management was underscored in several fundamental multi-edition monographs, for example, (Williams 2002; Kerzner 2009, 2017; Wysocki 2019).

The first example illustrating the "complexity of the research on complexity" goes deeply into the history of development of complexity-related studies. Waddington (1977, p. 30) observed: "no one has yet succeeded in giving a definition of 'complexity' which is meaningful enough to enable one to measure exactly how complex a system is". It could be expected that the development of mathematical modelling would lead to a better understanding of the phenomena put under the umbrella of complexity. However, a few years later, the impossibility of defining complexity was reiterated in a book with contributors including the "founding fathers" of the studies of complexity – Stuart Kauffman, John Holland, and Brian Arthur. The Preface begins with a humble statement: "Complexity is almost a theological concept; many people talk about it, but nobody knows what 'it' really is" (Stein 1989, p. xiii). It is also visible in the scheme illustrating the development of the research on complexity and chaos (Castellani 2018; Castellani and Gerrits 2021). The present time perspective allows to conclude that only developing descriptive definitions enumerating the characteristics (dimensions) of complexity seems reasonable.

The multitude of definitions and interpretations of complexity creates a situation of informational redundancy and noise which undermines theoretical considerations and the applicability of those concepts. Analysis of the links between Agile Project Management and complexity faces an additional specific dual obstacle. It is necessary to cope both with the fuzziness of definitions and interpretations of Agile Project Management, and the absence of commonly accepted typologies of interpretations of complexity in project management.

The above considerations show that any typological attempts may not focus on definitions of complexity. Instead, a less precise term is used – the interpretation of complexity. The interpretation of complexity is understood as an attempt to describe any non-decomposable collective object comprised of multiple interactive elements or phenomena – process, behaviour – abstract, physical, biological, and social with a collection of variously defined characteristics. These characteristics could be mathematical (quantitative) or verbal (qualitative) or mixed. By no means is this typological approach designed as the search for Weberian ideal types (Weber 1949). It only reflects difficulties arising in any attempts to develop typologies of understanding of complexity. At the same time the proposed typology can be viewed as a simplified source of guidance in searching for more profound discussion on the links between complexity-related concepts and project management in a general sense and on Agile Project Management.

It is commonly known that a universal collection of characteristics of complexity does not exist. Characteristics of complexity are defined/described in various domains of knowledge and they are called here complexity-related terms. In consequence, the assumptions of the proposed typology are as follows:

1) Inspiration from widely known and accepted typologies of interpretations of complexity-related concepts in a universal sense, in social sciences, in management, and in project management.
2) Awareness of the limitations of describing complexity in all domains of knowledge and in the studies of social systems in particular.
3) The necessity to collect and to systematize the interpretations of complexity and related ideas in project management where deepened studies of complexity, although quite numerous, are not yet as frequently found as in management. It would allow the theoretical foundations of project management broadly defined to be strengthened.
4) The necessity to deepen the knowledge about the role of complexity and related concepts in Agile Project Management where in some of the methodologies, e.g. Scrum or Adaptive System Development, complexity science plays a decisive role.
5) Time perspective allowing the main advantages and disadvantages of applications of complexity and akin ideas in software development and in project management to be identified and assessed. It concerns the applications which were originated 25 years ago (Agile Software Development and in Scrum).
6) Facilitating a deepened understanding of the role of complexity and associated ideas in the further development of Agile Project Management and in the applications of the idea of Agile beyond project management.

7) Awareness of the almost infinite profoundness of epistemological and methodological discussions on systems thinking and systems complexity in management reaching the philosophical foundation of science, e.g. Checkland (1999), Stacey and Mowles (2016), Jackson (2019).
8) Awareness of the impossibility of including all works on typology and all complexity-related domains. For example, understanding of operational research (OR) is purposively not discussed due to its broad scope. In addition, its role is mentioned in presenting ideas derived from and associated with OR – "hard" systems thinking, systems engineering.

The typology has several sources of inspiration. Although some of them are of a universal character, we focus our attention on ideas relating directly to social systems, to management, and to project management. In addition to the abovementioned typologies of interpretations of complexity, inspiration is also taken from Richardson and Cilliers (2001) who distinguish the following types of understanding of complexity in management theory: The "hard" complexity-related discussion labelled as complexity science or complexity theory (used here interchangeably with full awareness of subtleties which will be explained in the later considerations) similar to physics, chemistry, and biology based upon mathematical models, with the observer independent from the object of the study; and the "soft" complexity-related discussion, based upon metaphorical narratives, in which the observer is creating and observing the system. The last type is called "complexity thinking" and reflects the fact that in studying social systems, the limited and provisional nature of all understanding has to be recognized, both "hard" and "soft".

The concept of soft systems methodology, developed in opposition to hard systems engineering (Checkland 1999), also determines the divide between "hard" and "soft" projects proposed by Pollack (2007). However, it has to be borne in mind that Checkland's (1999) divide is not that simple – it is an engineering-like approach with an external observer and observer/participant.

The recent attempt by Yolles (2019) to define a hard-soft continuum (formal-informal) of interpretations of complexity also can be added to this collection of sources of inspiration and information in creating the proposed typology.

Two explanations have to be added so as to explain the sense of the proposal of a new typology of interpretations of complexity in project management: First, the role of the observer in interpretations of complexity, and second, mathematical models of complexity-related concepts and computability.

The role of the observer in studies of complexity is more intricate than it was proposed in "classical" systems thinking and cybernetics. The "hard" complexity is treated as an inherent feature of an entity (system), independent from the observer, i.e. "objective" as in the "first order cybernetics" (Wiener 1948/1961; Ashby 1957) and in General System Theory (von Bertalanffy 1968) and in other similar ideas described as systems thinking, systems approach, systems engineering, systems analysis, and systems dynamics.

The "soft" interpretations of complexity partly derive from "second order cybernetics" in which the role of observer is taken into account (von Foerster 1979, 1982, 2003). In "soft" complexity it is assumed that the object is not independent from the observer which is reflected in the famous observation "complexity as beauty is in the eyes of the beholder". It also means that it is necessary to study how the eye and the brain of the beholder operate.

This divide between "hard" and "soft" interpretations of complexity and the role of the observer is more intricate in a deeper epistemological analysis. In a qualitative narrative the role of the observer was included in theoretical reasoning by von Foerster (1979, 1982, 2003) in second-order cybernetics. It was also emphasized by Maturana and Varela (1980, p. 8) in the statement that everything said is said by an observer to an observer who could be self-observing. It means that a system and its complexity are subjective constructs. In consequence, according to constructivism (von Glasersfeld 1995), post-modernism (Cilliers 1998), and the interpretative approach (Tsoukas and Hatch 2001), any system must be treated as an intersubjective social construct created by observers/participants-observers in the process of their communication. This divide is somehow confirmed even when the ideas of "hard" and "soft" complexity of soft systems methodology are taken into account (Checkland 1999).

In the discussions on the universal meaning of complexity and on interpretations of complexity in physics, the specificity of relations between the observer and the observed in general considerations on complexity is also exposed: "Whatever complexity such systems have is a joint property of the system and its interaction with another system, most often an observer and/or controller" (Casti 1994, p. 269). It was also spelled out in the initial discussions on the mathematical modelling of complexity: "There are various quantities labeled 'complexity'. In each case, the complexity of a thing is context-dependent — in other words, dependent not only on the thing being described but also on who or what is doing the describing" (Gell-Mann 1994, p. 33). It must be added that we purposively do not delve into the subtleties of the role of observation in quantum mechanics.

In the interpretation of "hard" complexity as the domain of mathematical modelling, another key issue is computational complexity, its interpretations, and its limitations. In a crude approximation, computational complexity is usually associated with the limits of time and resources necessary for performing a specific task or with the length of the shortest message conveying certain information. These interpretations of complexity have been developed in different theoretical ideas such as algorithmic complexity, Kolmogorov complexity, Solomonoff-Kolmogorov-Chaitin complexity described in a synthetic study by Li and Vitányi (2008). Attempts have already been made to consider the challenges stemming from computational complexity in defining an interpretation of complexity in management (Moldoveanu 2004) and in the theory and practice of organizational structuration and in software development – an example is the development of Linux software (Moldoveanu and Bauer 2004, p. 111). In the era of development of artificial intelligence and sophisticated software, the barriers associated with computational complexity will influence the practice of designing, functioning, and developing software.

The above epistemological aspects of "hard" and "soft" complexity and computational complexity presented in a simplified way serve two purposes. Firstly, they are introduced so as to show the depth and scope of discussions on interpretations of complexity which also exert a strong impact on management and, subsequently, on project management. Secondly, they also can be treated as showing the direction of the studies of the links between various interpretations of complexity and Agile Project Management. The computational complexity is not included in the proposed typology of interpretations of complexity applied in project management. We only signal that awareness of computational complexity deserves more advanced further studies of software development theory and of the theoretical foundations of programming. References to the works of Moldoveanu are thus not incidental.

For the purpose of our study of interpretations of complexity-related concepts in project management we take into account three types of interpretations of complexity and of its characteristics: Hard, soft, and interpretations allowing for mixed characteristics.

The hard interpretations of complexity embody only mathematical models/simulation models that can be built with the use of tangible characteristics. It seems necessary to remember the meaning of tangibility in the studies of social systems. It can be explained with the properties of measurement. The Stevens (1946) scales of measurement have to be recalled, with full awareness of their weaknesses. First, tangibility embodies unequivocally defined physical properties of social systems measured with the Stevens ratio scale. Second, it also means that intersubjectively constructed characteristics of social systems can be operationalized/measured with the "hard" or "objective" Stevens ratio scale, e.g. costs, profits, or at least, a cardinal scale, e.g. different types of ranking and scoring, etc. The final tangible description of any social system is a combination of both components.

The soft interpretations embody qualitative, non-measurable descriptions. A closer look at the divide between "hard" and "soft" complexity leads to the conclusion that the "soft" complexity ideas do not exclude possibilities of operationalization. The borderline between them is sometimes unclear as was already mentioned in the concept of "complexity thinking" of Richardson and Cilliers (2001). This means that the delineation between hard and soft is an arbitrary divide of the continuum of interpretations.

A specific approach has been identified in the studies of already existing typologies of complexity associated with project management. It concerns the terms complexity of projects and complexity in projects. While in the above study (Maylor *et al.* 2008) no clear distinction is made between complexity in projects and complexity of projects – they are treated as interchangeable, in a later work, Geraldi *et al.* (2011, p. 968) state that complexity in projects embodies the studies of projects through the lenses of various complexity theories while complexity of projects is practitioner-driven and aims to identify the characteristics of complex projects and how individuals and organizations respond to this complexity.

In another approach, referring to the concept of complex responsive processes of relating (CRPR) in organizations developed by (Stacey *et al.* 2000, pp. 186–190) and with constructivism, the term "complexity in projects" is treated as an idea, a construct different from an object which can be reified. It comprises three aspects (Cicmil *et al.* 2009):

1) Persistent ambiguity and equivocality of project goals and contradictory and conflicting understandings of project success resulting in an on-going process of negotiation and re-evaluation of the project's purpose, goals, and performance among project participants.
2) The inherent unpredictability of future events, actions, responses and behaviours, time-flux, and change, which exposes the paradox of project control and the emergent nature of collaborative project work among participants enacting the project plan.
3) Complex multi-agency interfaces, social interaction, and processes of relating among project actors with different professional backgrounds, cultures, logics of representation, value systems, and positions of power, collaboratively constructing their local project rationality as a medium for joint action.

Remembering this duality, we leave the role of the CRPR in studies of complexity in project management for explanation in the next part of this book. For the sake of simplicity of the proposed typology, we apply the term complexity of projects because it dominates in the language of the theory and practice of project management. This discrepancy must be borne in mind whenever the constructivist character of projects is underscored.

As a novelty helpful in studying the role of complexity-related ideas in project management including APM, we add the intuitive interpretation of complexity. It has not been yet scrutinized in the general discussions on complexity, in management and in project management. The idea of intuitive interpretation of complexity placed between perfect order and absolute disorder was proposed by Heylighen (1999) and partially echoed in the early stages of development of Cynefin (Kurtz and Snowden 2003; Mikkelsen 2016). Our interpretations are more detailed, and we try to present the basic characteristics of any collectivity which are commonly treated as causing the use of the terms complex and/or complexity by the observer.

The introduction of this type of interpretations of complexity derives from a specific phenomenon observed in project management. In the works on project management, published when the ideas from systems thinking, cybernetics, and complexity science were already well-known, there were and still are works in which the interpretations of complexity are developed without direct reference to those ideas. As an example, the work of (Baccarini 1996) can be recalled. The interpretations of that kind of complexity and their applications were systematized by (Maylor *et al.* 2008).

Special attention in our research and in developing our typology was given to two comprehensive typological approaches to complexity in project management. The first was developed by Manfred Saynisch and his co-workers in their theoretical and practice-oriented project called Project Management Second Order (PM-2). The project is discussed in Chapter 5, so here only a few remarks about the typology of complexity-related ideas in Saynisch's project are given. It was also used as partial inspiration in our study. Our typologies are partly overlapping, and there are areas of complexity-related studies which are different. While Saynisch's approach is more oriented towards practice, with some necessary simplification, our approach is oriented towards theory and applications, with more attention paid to deepened theoretical considerations. We illustrate our theoretical discussion with selected examples developed by other authors and at the same time, according to the aim of our project, our typology of interpretations of complexity-related ideas can be helpful in advanced applications of these ideas in project management in a general sense and in Agile Project Management.

The second typology, elaborated recently by Mikkelsen (2020), embodies five ideal research types of complexity:

- Positivistic modelling (search for prediction based on law-like relations)
- Complexity theory (search for an explanation of the unpredictable behaviour of projects)
- Ontological framework (search for a comprehensive description of project complexity)
- Managerial framework (designing prescriptive theory for handling project complexity)
- Emancipative framework (project cases – without the intention of generalization)

This typology is treated as another example of ordering of interpretations of complexity. They are more universal, but at the same time they reduce the application of broadly defined complexity theory-based research only to the unpredictable behaviour of projects. Such an approach seems to be a significantly simplified interpretation of complexity theory/complexity science.

Taking into account the conclusions deriving from the above discussions, the proposed typology of interpretations of complexity in project management is built on a superposition of two criteria.

The first generic criterion constitutes a foundation for the identification of broadly defined domains of theory and practice in which hard and soft interpretations of complexity have been developed, i.e. cybernetics, systems thinking, complexity science, etc. Such a typology can never be complete, and the borderlines between types of interpretations can never be clearly marked.

This criterion does not create a unified pure type but rather a cluster of types. Table 3.1 can be viewed solely as a kind of introductory scheme to the further studies of the internal structure of the clusters of interpretations of complexity.

According to the second criterion two types can be distinguished. Hard interpretations of complexity can be described with more or less advanced mathematical models (simulation models). Soft qualitative interpretations embody two sub-types: Pure qualitative characteristics of complexity and mixed, quantitative and qualitative interpretations. As was stated, the clear-cut distinction between hard and soft complexity is sometimes difficult to mark unequivocally, and the type of interpretation will be additionally explained when discussing specific interpretations.

In the first step of developing the typology, a database of publications has been created including major publications: Books, a broad variety of journals and conference materials as well as specialized selected websites in which complexity and complexity-related ideas were applied in universally understood

Table 3.1 Typology of interpretations of complexity-related concepts in project management

Hard interpretations of complexity **Quantitative characteristics Mathematical models (simulation models)**	**Intuitive complexity**	**Soft interpretations of complexity** **Purely qualitative characteristics** **Mixed quantitative and qualitative characteristics**
	Cybernetics	
	• First-order cybernetics	
	• Managerial cybernetics	
	• Second-order cybernetics	
	General Systems Theory	
	Sociocybernetics	
	Quantitative systems modelling	
	• System dynamics	
	• Systems analysis	
	• Systems engineering	
	Modern system thinking	
	• Soft systems thinking	
	• Critical systems thinking	
	• System of Systems Methods	
	Complexity science	
	• Chaos theory and non-linearity	
	• Non-equilibrium thermodynamics	
	• Complex adaptive systems	
	• Cellular automata	
	• Edge of chaos	
	• Scale-free networks	
	• Synergetics (Herman Haken)	
	• Catastrophe theory	
	Wicked problems	
	Synergetics (Buckminster Fuller)	
	Hierarchies, holons, and fractal organization	
	Social systems of Niklas Luhmann	

Source: Own research.

non-Agile project management. The database also includes works with applications of complexity and complexity-related ideas in Agile methodological frameworks in software development and in project management. Due to the necessity of careful interpretations of variously defined terms, the automatized methods of text mining were not necessary at this stage of research. The results of our research can be used in further specialized, more focused research.

The number of works on complexity-related ideas in management and in project management is astounding. In addition, to make the typological ordering efforts even more arduous, the same characteristics of complexity can be assigned to various typological categories, e.g. non-linearity which belongs to chaos theory, complex adaptive systems, and non-equilibrium thermodynamics. Therefore, in presenting the typology of interpretations of complexity, we present only introductory information needed for further studies. Some descriptions are minimized and some less well-known ideas are added.

The variety of interpretations of the complexity of social systems makes it impossible to prepare their typology in a more or less unequivocal way. In the case of applications in project management, we have, as usual, somehow arbitrarily to separate a group labelled as indigenous complexity-related concepts. They are differentiated and although common features with other interpretations can be found, e.g. the ideas of Niklas Luhmann and second order cybernetics, they are treated separately. The role of fractals in project management also requires additional explanation. Fractals are predominantly connected with chaos theory, but the variety of applications of this theory in project management is quite broad. However, this is not the only reason to consider their role in projects separately. The second reason for placing separately the applications of fractal-related ideas in project management is that they are usually studied together with hierarchical projects.

Every type of interpretation of complexity in project management is identified according to the following scheme:

1) A brief description of the domain of complexity-related studies, e.g. cybernetics, systems thinking, systems analysis, complexity science.
2) Description/definition/interpretation of complexity developed in this domain, e.g. complexity in system dynamics.
3) Complexity-related concepts developed in this domain, e.g. feedback and the law of requisite variety in cybernetics.
4) Examples from project management applying complexity-related concepts from the domain under scrutiny, e.g. methodologies from project management in which feedback and the law of requisite variety are used.
5) Examples from Agile Project Management. Depending on the typological category and importance they are only briefly mentioned and a more detailed description of such applications is presented in the part of the book devoted to detailed studies of specific methodological approaches to Agile and complexity.

6) The order of subsequent subchapters is almost fully mirrored in the sequence of subchapters with some minor exceptions resulting from considering other criteria.
7) Last but not least, the interpretations of concepts associated with complexity are presented in likely scores of thousands of works and in likely a similar number of more or less competent websites. That is why the description of the types of interpretations is reduced to a necessary minimum and relevant reference sources are presented. Exceptions have been made for less well-known and/or older ideas and sources.

Agile Project Management and intuitive interpretations of complexity

The first attempts to study systematically and to define more precisely the intuitive features of complexity were made in the works of Weaver (1948) – organized and unorganized complexity – and Simon (1962, 1973, 1995) – complexity, hierarchy, and near decomposability.

The idea of intuitive complexity proposed here is partly inspired by two comments on the attempts to define complexity made by Simon. The first (Simon 1962, pp. 467–468):

> I shall not undertake a formal definition of "complex systems." Roughly, by a complex system I mean one made up of a large number of parts that interact in a non-simple way. In such systems, the whole is more than the sum of the parts, not in an ultimate, metaphysical sense, but in the important pragmatic sense that, given the properties of the parts and the laws of their interaction, it is not a trivial matter to infer the properties of the whole.

The second (Simon 1995, p. 26): We can regard a system as complex if it can be analyzed into many components having relatively many relations among them, so that the behavior of each component depends on the behavior of the others. That definition embraces a very large number of the systems in nature in which we are interested, ranging from molecules and microbes, to mammals and metropolises and megapowers.

The following distinctive features allow the interpretation of the notion of complexity to be treated as intuitive (quantitative "hard", qualitative "soft", and the mixed interpretations):

- Description of complexity with universal characteristics commonly treated as intuitive, e.g. number of elements, differentiation of elements and their states, number and characteristics of internal interactions, internal hierarchy of the system (functional hierarchy, structural hierarchy, power hierarchy, containment hierarchy – structural complexity), number and characteristics of interactions between the system (collectivity) with the environment.

- Dynamics of a collectivity (behaviour) depicted with simple intuitive quantitative and qualitative characteristics – speed of change of elements, of their internal interactions, and of the whole collectivity, growth, decay, dissipation.
- Applying the term complexity in relation to uncertainty and unpredictability in a quantitative and qualitative sense.
- Linking complexity with an insufficient amount of measurable information and difficulty with gathering that information.
- The use of the term complexity without any reference object (stand-alone) or in a sense which cannot be sufficiently precisely defined, e.g. complex thinking, complex development, complex behaviour, etc.
- Treating the interpretation of complexity as a point of departure for various methods of operationalization such as in system dynamics, system analysis, system engineering.
- Interpretating complexity as a countable noun, assuming that there exist various types of complexity, as in the above point; in such case the plural term complexities is justifiable.
- Applying the characteristics of complexity which had been defined earlier, independently from cybernetics, systems thinking, and complexity science, but which were later given more profound interpretations, definitions, and mathematical models, e.g. emergence, hierarchy, self-organization, synergy.

The idea of intuitive complexity has not been yet applied in the research referring to complexity. A survey of applications of this interpretation in systems analysis, in systems engineering, in management, and in project management leads to the conclusion that defining and studying this type of complexity is necessary because in many instances complexity and related terms are used in a purely intuitive sense.

There are multiple examples of applications of the intuitive quantitative interpretation of complexity in management. Daft (1992, p. 15) equates complexity with the number of activities or subsystems within the organization, noting that it can be measured along three dimensions. Vertical complexity is the number of levels in an organizational hierarchy, horizontal complexity is the number of job titles or departments across the organization, and spatial complexity is the number of geographical locations.

Intuitive interpretations of complexity are associated with the already mentioned complexity of projects as distinctive from complexity in projects (Cicmil *et al.* 2009).

The pioneering and frequently quoted work of Baccarini (1996) can be used as an example. It includes a comprehensive quantitative intuitive interpretation of complexity of projects. "Project complexity, depending on product complexity is consisting of many varied interrelated parts and can be operationalized in terms of differentiation and interdependency" (Baccarini 1996, pp. 202–203). The universal complexity of projects embodies organizational complexity and technological complexity. They are both defined by differentiation and interdependency, which, in turn, are characterized by intuitively defined measurable characteristics such as the number of levels of hierarchy, the number of organizational units, the degree of operational interdependencies, the number of actions, etc. Without delving into the details, it may be concluded that the complexity of projects is represented by measurable intuitive characteristics.

Cybernetics, General System Theory, and sociocybernetics

The presentation of definitions of complexity in cybernetics and systems thinking with a thorough but simplified study of primary sources allows all authors of Agile-related works to avoid superficial studies. So as to broaden the background, examples of applications of these ideas from "classical" cybernetics and systems thinking are quoted.

As was already mentioned, there are multiple, overlapping, and contradicting interpretations of the terms systems approach, systems philosophy, systems theory, General System Theory, and systems thinking. Their relations with cybernetics and its sub-domains are also not too clearly delineated (Principia Cybernetica Web). The present perspective on the history of cybernetics and systems thinking leads to the conclusion that any efforts aiming at the systematization of the research area are not necessary anymore. Bearing in mind this situation and the need for simplification for use in project management, we briefly present both hard and soft interpretations of complexity and complexity-related ideas developed in cybernetics, management cybernetics, and General System Theory and system thinking.

Cybernetics

First-order cybernetics

Cybernetics was developed as an inter- and even transdisciplinary domain of knowledge which was supposed to provide universal models of communication and control in all types of systems, beginning from physics and chemistry, through biology, and ending with social sciences, neurobiology, and psychology. The ideas of cybernetics are widely described in multiple works quoted in this part; thus we focus solely on the role of complexity-related ideas in cybernetics and its particular domains. There are various sub-domains of cybernetics: First-order cybernetics, second-order cybernetics, managerial cybernetics, and sociocybernetics, with the latter constituting a synthesis of various streams of cybernetics, systems thinking, and complexity science. The hard interpretations of complexity are associated predominantly with the first-order cybernetics in which the object is independent from the observer. As the founders of cybernetics, Gregory Bateson, Julian Bigelow, Warren McCulloch, Heinz von Foerster, Margaret Mead, Arturo Rosenblueth, John von Neumann, Walter Pitts, Claude Shannon, and Norbert Wiener are recognized as participants of the Macy Conferences in 1946–1953.

The works of Norbert Wiener (1948/1961) and W. Ross Ashby (1957) played a special role in developing theoretical thought concerning complexity-related ideas both in hard and soft interpretations. The name cybernetics was coined by Wiener with inspiration from the Greek κυβερνήτης (kybernetes) (Latin equivalent *gubernator*) – governor, steersman. It was designed to describe "the science of control and communication, in the animal and the machine" (Wiener 1948/1961). When cybernetics became popular, other earlier uses of the term cybernetics were recalled – Plato, Aristotle, Ampère, Trentowski (American Society for Cybernetics 2003; Trentowski 2020).

In the first book of Wiener (1948/1961) the term complexity was mentioned only in very general terms. References to complexity can be found in mathematical models illustrating such concepts as feedback, information, communication, learning, non-linearity, self-organization, and self-reproducing machines. Wiener in his mathematical models relating to cybernetics in the first book (Wiener 1948) did not try to directly link his models with complexity. In the second book, presenting his reflections on the impact of cybernetics on society, he uses the terms complex and complexity but without any detailed explanation; thus they can be assigned to two types – soft intuitive complexity and soft intuitive, cybernetics-related complexity. The examples include the complex nature of communications, complex ideas, complex codes of human communication, and complex data (Wiener 1954).

In his fundamental book, Ashby (1957) treated complexity as the key distinctive feature of such systems as the brain, computing machines, human organism, and society and declared that his research aimed at developing methods of studying them as complex systems. Complexity was described with heterogeneity in the parts, and great richness of connexion and internal interaction (Ashby 1958, p. 11). Looking from the present point of view it may be concluded that Ashby's definition of complexity reflected intuitive complexity, the interpretations proposed by Weaver (1948) and Shannon's information theory (Shannon and Weaver 1949).

Cybernetics was defined by Ashby as providing effective methods for the study, and control, of systems that are intrinsically extremely complex. Due to their complexity they can be treated as black boxes with full or limited observability of their behaviour, without knowing their internal processes and structures. In his works he developed a multitude of measures and models allowing the depiction of the universal complexity of those systems using such concepts as adaptation, change, feedback, equilibrium, Shannon's information, stability, regulation, and ultrastability.

The main ideas of Ashby include the homeostat, the law of requisite variety, the principle of self-organization, and the principle of regulatory models. According to the Principia Cybernetica Web, Ashby can be counted as a forerunner of the idea of complex adaptive systems. One of the most influential ideas associated with complex systems was the law of requisite variety stating that variety in regulating system can force down the variety in the subject of regulation. In other words, variety can destroy variety (Ashby 1957, p. 209).

Two ideas reflect the complexity of controlling and controlled system. The first one is the law of requisite variety and the second, circular causality. The controller affects the controlled system and the feedback from the controlled affects the controlled in a circular process or in a loop (Scott 2021, p. 7). Boisot and McKelvey (2011, p. 279) proposed an extension of the law of requisite variety into the law of requisite complexity which holds that, to be efficaciously adaptive, the internal complexity of a system must match the external complexity it confronts.

It must be added that, in the time of the dominance of terminology borrowed from complexity science in its hard, mathematical form and as the foundation of multiple metaphors, e.g. chaos, the edge of chaos, etc., it is sometimes forgotten how strongly first-order cybernetics influenced the language of management, and subsequently, of project management. The terms adaptation, black box, control, feedback (negative and positive), homeostat, homeostasis, equilibrium, and stability as well as the first definitions of complexity constitute since then an indispensable component of their vocabulary.

First-order cybernetics remained a significant source of inspiration, theoretical background, and practice of dealing with complexity-related problems in project management. It demands more systematic studies but an introductory survey shows a strong impact of the law of requisite variety. A few examples from the many can be recalled. The influential paper of Anbari (1985) is well-known for setting the objectives/constraints of project management: Scope, quality, time, and cost. It is less known that, in the same paper, Anbari, treating projects as complex systems in a universal sense, without detailed descriptions, proposed to extend the law of requisite variety with time perspective. The proposal was of a qualitative character although building mathematical models was also suggested. As a more recent example of linking the law of requisite variety and Agile Project Management, Emma Sharrock's (2015) book is worth recalling.

Heinz von Foerster: Second-order cybernetics and self-organization

In the first-order cybernetics proposed by Wiener and Ashby and their followers, the object of observation was predominantly treated as independent from the observer. This distinction is a simplification and demands additional explanation. For Ashby, a psychiatrist by background, in the initial works, the dominant cognitive posture was an engineering-like approach separating the observer from the observed in the studies of all types of systems. However, in his later work on self-organization, Ashby declares that properties derive from relations between observer and thing (Ashby 1962, p. 258).

A new, universal approach was proposed by Heinz von Foerster in 1974 (von Foerster 1979, 1982, 2003; Scott 2021) who extended the studies in cybernetics with the self-reference and self-reflexivity of the observer. According to von Foerster first-order cybernetics is the study of observed systems while second-order cybernetics is the study of observing systems. He also referred to this second domain as cybernetics of cybernetics (von Foerster 1979). On the ground of systems studies the ideas of von Foerster corresponded with the role of observer exposed in the famous observation of Maturana and Varela. It is thus natural that second-order cybernetics is closely related to social constructivism in its radical form promoted by von Glasersfeld (1995). Von Foerster also added to Maturana and Varela (1980, p. 8) proposition: "anything said is said by an observer", his own "corollary": "Anything said is said to an observer" (von Foerster 1979, p. 5) thus highlighting the fact that conclusions from observations are constructed in language and for people capable of observation.

Following Ashby and other cyberneticians von Foerster studies the phenomenon of self-organization. He developed his own theory of self-organization deriving from thermodynamics and information theory. In his concept self-organization results from informational noise in the system (von Foerster 1960). Remembering this interpretation is necessary in further considerations on self-organization in Agile Project Management.

The picture of cybernetics as the source of inspiration for project management and Agile Project Management in particular would not be complete without presenting the contribution of Gordon Pask. His cybernetical ideas are less known even in the community of systems researchers but more profound research allows the discovery of a broad variety of his multiple innovative ideas. In consequence of the aim of our study and obvious limitations we present briefly only selected ideas of Pask depicted in his publications and in the works of authors describing his contribution to cybernetics (Pask 1969, 1975, 1975a, 1976; Pickering 2010; Jackson 2019; Scott 2021).

The scope of Pask's contribution to cybernetics is quite broad and includes cybernetics and arts, adaptive training and teaching machines, learning and education, chemical computers, the epistemology of cybernetics, conversation theory, and its extension -interactions of actors theory and cybernetics of architecture and design.

Conversation theory resulted from Pask's interests in the psychology of learning, especially with the use of simple machines (when seen from the current perspective). Pask treated the interaction between the learned and the learning as complex conversation. A deepening understanding of communicative interaction proposed in the conversation theory can be helpful for a better understanding of social systems (Pask 1975, 1975a; Pickering 2010; Scott 2021, pp. 23–29) built on interpersonal communication. From the point of view of project management, the main contribution of Pask were the concepts drawn from cybernetics to theory of architectural design (Pask 1969). The main ideas put forward in the paper concentrate on the following features of architectural design: A holistic approach, evolutionary ideas in architecture, symbolic environments in architecture, building as a system and thus the construction of a building must be treated as a system, and taking cybernetics as a universal theory of architecture.

The proposed approach to architecture is summarized in a simple cybernetic design paradigm referring to the context of a reactive and adaptive environment. The paradigm embodies the following interdependent stages (Pask 1969, p. 496):

1) Specification of the purpose or goal of the system (with respect to the human inhabitants). It should be emphasized that the goal may be and nearly always will be underspecified, i.e. the architect will no more know the purpose of the system than he really knows the purpose of a conventional house.
2) Choice of the basic environmental materials.
3) Selection of the invariants which are to be programmed into the system. Partly at this stage and partly in (2) above, the architect determines what properties will be relevant in the man-environment dialogue.
4) Specification of what the environment will learn about and how it will adapt.
5) Choice of a plan for adaptation and development. In case the goal of the system is underspecified, as in (1), the plan will chiefly consist in a number of evolutionary principles.

Pask's cybernetical ideas were used in developing the links between design theory and cybernetics. As an inspiring example the concept of Dubberly and Pangaro (2015) can be quoted. They present a synthesis approach to design linking second-order cybernetics with conversation theory. Their approach can be illustrated with the following scheme (Dubberly and Pangaro 2015, p. 63):

- If design, then systems
- If systems, then cybernetics
- If cybernetics, then second-order cybernetics
- If second-order cybernetics, then conversation

The key role in transferring cybernetics-based knowledge to management was played by Stafford Beer. Leaving aside his multiple ideas and achievements – see Pickering (2010) – we focus here only on his contribution to the development of the concepts relating to complexity. The interpretations of complexity proposed by Beer derive partly from his experience in operations research, and although some of them are quantitative and some qualitative they are all included in hard complexity developed from the inspiration taken from cybernetics. For the first time Beer defined various types of complex systems in his book *Cybernetics and Management* (Beer 1957). Using two criteria – the first, the degree of simplicity and the second, complexity and prediction-oriented: Deterministic and probabilistic, Beer (1957, p. 18) presents three examples of complex deterministic systems: An electronic digital computer, a planetary system, and automation. Complex probabilistic systems are the following: Stockholding, conditioned reflexes, and industrial profitability. He declared the economy, the brain, and the company to be exceedingly complex systems which must be probabilistic.

A comprehensive concept embodying the capabilities of organization and all types of social systems operating in a complex environment called the Viable System Model (VSM) was described by Beer in a series of books (Beer 1972, 1979, 1981) and promoted by other authors (e.g. Espejo and Harnden 1989; Espejo 2009). The key feature of the VSM is the management of complexity expressed with the variety of the environment and the variety of the organization. The system is viable if it can respond to the changes in the environment whether or not they have been predicted. The system must achieve the requisite variety imposed by its complex environment. The essence of the viability presented in the VSM can be depicted with the following characteristics:

- Autonomous biological or social system
- Survival in the changing environment as the main goal of the system
- Learning and adaptation as instruments of survival
- Hierarchical recursive structure – a viable system is an element of a viable system

Beer referred to complexity directly and indirectly in his later works. In the essay on the role of computers in management, he treated complexity as the main attribute of social life and as the main factor determining the management of organizations. Probabilistic complexity was pictured as a result of a growing number of interactions in the systems in which self-control and self-organization constitute the management principle thanks to which the systems grow and are stable, learn and adjust, adapt and evolve. The growth of complexity was connected with the growing capacity of data-handling and the information explosion. The latter argument seems especially important. This phenomenon which is regarded as crucial for the Information Society was raised by Beer already in the 1970s.

Beer's ideas on complexity were also related to other concepts, including *autopoiesis* of Maturana and Varela (1980). In his Presidential Address to the Triennial Congress of the World Organization of Systems and Cybernetics, New Delhi, India, January 1993 (Beer 1993), he underscored the need for a better understanding of the complexity of global problems. Complexity can be measured with variety. In consequence, the number of internal relationships in a complex system grows exponentially with the linear growth of the system. It is even more intricate because the development of technology contributes to exploding variety where the exponential function is itself an exponent. Beer authored other comprehensive concepts of management directly and indirectly connected with complexity.

The idea of organization of human meetings called Team Syntegrity inspired by R. Buckminster Fuller's architectonic principle of efficiency in the design of specific constructions – geodesic domes occupies a special place in the scientific output of Beer. Buckminster Fuller analysed the peculiar properties of those domes with the idea of tensile integrity, or "tensegrity" for short. Subsequently Beer adopted the suggestion that his approach should be called "Team Syntegrity", once more invoking the notion of synergy (Beer 1994, pp. 13–14).

This format for holding the meeting called syntegration has to be organized according to the structure of a very specific geometric polyhedral figure icosahedron treated by Buckminster Fuller as one of the core element geodesic domes (Fuller 1997; Beer 1994). The icosahedron reflects the discussion of 30 participants of about 12 topics. The main idea behind the use of the icosahedron as a pattern for the organization of human teams in collective problem solving was that the sources of optimal organization of human activities can be found in nature. Leaving aside further explanations it can be added that syntegration was designed not only as an instrument for the collective solving of management problems but of multiple types of human problems at all levels of societal hierarchy.

The VSM was initially designed for increasing the effectiveness of corporate management but also to enhance and to improve the effectiveness of the organizational design. From multiple examples the following ones can be quoted. Piney (2008) proposed the concept of probernetics, a new methodology based on the VSM which was supposed to be helpful in dealing with complexity in project management. The VSM has been recently applied in the assessment of software development projects but without any special dedication to Agile Project Management (Puche-Regaliza *et al.* 2020). Because of the increasing role of sustainability in project management the applications of the VSM in this area of theory and practice are also worth mentioning as insightful for project management (Espinosa and Walker 2017). The ideas of Beer's associated with the VSM and with syntegrity are included in research, training, and consulting by the Cwarel Isaf Institute in Switzerland.

A special application of Beer's ideas was Project Cybersyn (cybernetic synergy), a project which was designed to govern the economy of Chile under President Salvador Allende. The project was terminated after the collapse of the government of President Allende in 1973, but it is recalled in multiple writings as the largest attempt so far to use the ideas drawn from cybernetics at the national scale (Beer 1981; Espejo 2009; Pickering 2010; Jackson 2019).

General System Theory

The origins and development of cybernetics in the late 1940s and the 1950s coincided with the beginnings of another scientific approach to studying all types of complex systems, beginning from the atomic level and ending with astronomy. This new approach was developed parallelly to cybernetics by scholars from different disciplines: Ludwig von Bertalanffy (theoretical biology), Kenneth Boulding (economics), and Anatol Rapoport (mathematics, theoretical biology, philosophy), to mention the most influential figures. A comprehensive vision of this new idea called General System Theory was presented in a synthetic way in the book of von Bertalanffy (1968). It must be added, what is often omitted in the later writings, that General System Theory was designed as a mathematical universal theory of systems in nature and in society. The key idea of General System Theory is a universal, holistic concept of systems described as "complexes of elements standing in interactions" (von Bertalanffy 1968, p. 33). Von Bertalanffy argued that physical systems are closed systems while the biological systems are open systems interacting with their environment and adapting to its changes. An open system was defined as a system in exchange of matter with its environment, presenting import and export, building-up and breaking-down of its material components.

Von Bertalanffy (1968, pp. 124–153) discerned the following characteristics of open systems:

1) Open systems can be represented by mathematical models describing their fundamental characteristics.
2) Steady state is opposite to equilibrium: The system remains constant in its composition, in spite of continuous irreversible processes, import and export, building-up and breaking-down, taking place.
3) Equifinality: The same final state can be reached from different initial conditions and even after disturbances of the process.
4) From the viewpoint of thermodynamics, open systems can maintain themselves in a state of high statistical improbability, of order and organization.
5) An open system may come to a higher level of ordering through acquiring information.

General System Theory by definition was regarded as inter- and multi-disciplinary and included ideas borrowed from various domains of science, e.g. biology, information theory, game theory, net theory, computer simulation. It also aimed at the unification of science. The universal isomorphic systemic properties were treated as not reducible and relevant to a broad variety of systems grouped in a hierarchy of systems, beginning from static structures, atoms, and molecules and ending with socio-cultural systems and symbolic systems (Boulding 1956).

In the first works on General System Theory references were predominantly made to the ideas of disorganized complexity and organized complexity of Weaver (1948) with the former being studied in thermodynamics and the latter as a potential area of studies by General System Theory. It is also necessary to mention that although General System Theory was defined as distinct from cybernetics, the impact of ideas from cybernetics, especially feedback, control, and homeostasis, were referred to by von Bertalanffy (1968). To strengthen the institutional position of system studies, Bertalanffy and his co-researchers established in 1956 the Society for General System Theory which in 1957 changed its name to "Society for General Systems Research" (SGSR).

When presenting the role of the founders of systems studies it is necessary to underscore that they initiated one of most important scientific areas of the 20th century. It must be added that the initial attempts to study systems within more systematic borders were not successful. At present we realize that putting in order all the ideas linked by the term system such as systems thinking, system approach, systems theory (non-incidental use of plural of the term system), systems studies, and systemology constitutes an unsurmountable goal. In the majority of the works on systems studies no attempts are made to order the ideas. As an example, the typology of Castellani (2018), and Castellani and Gerrits (2021) can be mentioned. It shows the relations and only a very broad ordering. To put some order into our discussions concerning all the ideas stemming from the General System intellectual movement we will use the term systems thinking.

These remarks are purposively made as a kind of warning to all theoreticians and practitioners who are discovering (or re-discovering) the usefulness of the abovementioned ideas drawn from systems thinking, or whatever we may call them in project management, and in Agile Project Management in particular. When searching for inspiration in complexity-related ideas we have to realize how complex they are due to the multitude of interpretations.

Direct references to the ideas of General System Theory and related abovementioned concepts are not quite common in the literature on project management. Kerzner (2009, p. 38) mentions General Systems Theory and von Bertalanffy and Boulding as its authors although without any formal bibliographical entries. In the 12th edition of his textbook Kerzner (2017, pp. 79–82) describes systems approach and systems thinking interchangeably but without any reference to specific sources. This situation can be explained by the growing popularity of applications of systems thinking in management and in project management.

Sociocybernetics

The importance of cybernetics was already confirmed by Wiener (1954) and it is something common. When studying the impact of cybernetics on social sciences, including management and project management, it is worthwhile to mention sociocybernetics, a proposal of the scientific domain unifying cybernetics and all streams of systems studies. Sociocybernetics was initiated by Felix Geyer and Johannes van der Zouwen in the 1970s and developed in the 1980s and 1990s (Scott 2021). Sociocybernetics was designed as a specific synthesis of all domains of systems studies which could provide new insights into sociology. It was defined by its authors as (Geyer and van der Zouwen 1992, p. 95):

> the application of concepts, methods, and ideas of the so-called new cybernetics or second-order cybernetics to the study of social and sociocultural systems, but also vice versa: second-order cybernetics is certainly enriched by the often unexpected results of social science studies in which the concepts of second-order cybernetics are applied.

As the main contributions of sociocybernetics to social studies the following ideas were regarded as most important for social studies (Geyer 1995):

1) First-order cybernetics: Boundaries of the system, structure of the system (system, subsystem, and suprasystem), positive and negative feedback (circular causality).
2) Second-order cybernetics (observation, self-observation, *autopoiesis*, limits of control of natural systems).

This framework definition has been extended by including the areas associated with almost all areas of complex systems studies (e.g. Scott 2021). Sociocybernetics addressed predominantly the universal problems of society but at present the scope of interest of sociocybernetics is much broader.

System dynamics, systems analysis, and systems engineering

The need for the effective design, study, and managing of variously defined complex engineering and socio-technical systems gave birth to three methodological approaches which originated under the influence of cybernetics, systems thinking, and operational research: System dynamics, systems analysis, and systems engineering. Their main common denominator was an engineering-like approach to complexity with the domination of "hard" quantitative modelling and simulation.

System dynamics

The main concepts of system dynamics are rooted in cybernetics. Jay Forrester is usually declared as its key founder but there were also other engineers who turned their attention to management and economics (Stacey and Mowles 2016, p. 58). System dynamics is an example of linking systems thinking with mathematical models including positive and negative feedback as the characteristics of complexity. The mathematical models are used as a foundation of simulation models. The interpretation of complexity used in system dynamics can be assigned to intuitive quantitative complexity, to quantitative complexity developed in systems thinking (feedback), and indirectly to complexity science (non-linear models). Frequently the process of operationalization of complexity begins from quantitative intuitive complexity which is operationalized differently. System dynamics has been applied in studying various social systems – companies (business strategy), urban planning, and world models (Forrester 1961, 1975). As an additional contribution of Forrester to the studies of complexity the concept of counterintuitive behaviour of social systems can be mentioned (Forrester 1971).

System dynamics has also become an important instrument of project management. It is the core of complexity of projects developed by Williams (1999, 2002, pp. 50–58, 2005). Following Baccarini (1996) he distinguished two dimensions of complexity in project management. Purely quantitative complexity – structural complexity, deriving from the number of elements and interdependency relating to product and subsequently, to project and uncertainty, embodying uncertainty in goals and uncertainty in methods. It is necessary to reiterate that in both cases, even in the paper aiming at searching for new paradigms for complex projects (Williams 1999), no reference was made to any precisely defined complexity, should it be cybernetics, systems thinking, or complexity science. A reference was only made to the ideas drawn from systems dynamics – the works of Forrester.

Systems analysis

Independently from systems thinking, the concept of engineering-like systems analysis embodying project management was developed in the USA by the RAND Corporation, initially only for military purposes. The definitions of complexity were connected to specific intuitive interpretations and Weaver's organized complexity. The scope and evolution of complexity-oriented methodology in the RAND studies can be illustrated with three examples. From "hard" engineering-like interpretations of complexity applied by RAND and later also by the International Institute of Applied Systems Analysis (IIASA) in Austria (established during *la détente* between the USA and the USSR in the Cold War) (Miser and Quade 1985) through similar but more methodologically advanced approaches (Drezner 2009) and ending with the methodological proposals built on the complex sdaptive Systems and suggesting an increased role of qualitative methodologies as more suitable for dealing with complex projects (Davis *et al.* 2020).

An important observation was made by Williams (2005). It concerns the roots of the normative approaches in project management expressed in the Project Management Body of Knowledge (PMBoK) prepared by the Project Management Institute. In his opinion, the concepts of the PMBoK are conceptually grounded in the works of Cleland and King (1967, 1983). Without a deeper analysis of consequences of this opinion for the present PMBoK standards and looking from the present point of view, it can be confirmed that the understanding of complexity in the PMI standards is deeply rooted in quantitative complexity as defined in the early development of system dynamics (as mentioned above) and in systems analysis.

Systems engineering

Systems engineering also originated as a methodological framework designated to deal with complex engineering systems. The first ideas which can be called systems engineering were proposed in the 1940s but the full development of systems engineering could be observed from the 1950s. Like system analysis, systems engineering was initially designated for military purposes in the USA. Focusing attention on the interpretations of complexity, it may be stated that in the early period of development of systems engineering complexity was treated as a simple result of the number of elements of engineering systems and the number of their relations (Hall 1962). Systems engineering constitutes at present a strong intellectual and institutional area of systems research and includes several knowledge areas, as for example (*Guide to the Systems Engineering* 2021): Product Systems Engineering (PSE), Enterprise Systems Engineering (ESE), Service Systems Engineering (SSE).

Referring to a large number of information sources concerning systems engineering, e.g. International Council on Systems Engineering (INCOSE), *MITRE Systems Engineering Guide* (2014), *Guide to the Systems Engineering Body of Knowledge (SEBoK)* (2021), and several publications (e.g. Boppana *et al.* 2008), it may be concluded that hard, intuitive, and cybernetics-based ideas of complexity dominated in the earlier periods of development of system engineering. At present a strong impact of ideas deriving from complexity science on systems engineering is also observed (Bar-Yam 2003). It should be also underlined that the broadly defined Agile approach to software development, project management, and management in general has become popular in systems engineering developed by leading institutions applying broadly defined systems engineering (*MITRE Systems Engineering Guide* 2014).

Summing up the above ideas of dealing with complex systems it may be concluded that systems analysis and systems engineering have different conceptual institutional origins but in the process of their development the approach to complexity has become to a large extent similar, if not identical.

Soft systems methodology, critical systems thinking, and System of Systems Methodologies

Two below described domains of systems studies have common roots in the holistic ideas of General Systems Theory of Ludvig von Bertalanffy, Kenneth Boulding, and Anatol Rapoport. At the same time they are critical of reductionist approaches used in operational research and systems engineering. They offer various alternatives, extensions, and syntheses of systems methodological frameworks aiming at synthetic approaches to complex socio-engineering systems. Due to a very broad range of methods and ideas only a limited number of examples drawn from project management and Agile Project Management are quoted as illustrations of applications of the ideas drawn from SSM and critical systems thinking.

Soft systems methodology

Soft systems methodology (SSM) was developed by Peter Checkland and his co-researchers as a reaction to the limitations of systems engineering and reductionism but at the same time as a continuation and extension of the classical General Systems Theory of von Bertalanffy, Boulding, and Rapoport. It originated in the late 1960s within the action research programme at the University of Lancaster. Soft systems methodology was for the first time described by Checkland in 1981. Subsequently, more works were published and here only selected works are recalled: Checkland and Scholes (1990) and Checkland (1999). It must be added that Checkland's publication of 1999 includes *in extenso* the book of 1981.

The main determinants of developing soft system methodology can be summarized as follows. In classical systems theory, in systems engineering, and in OR the system under scrutiny was independent from the observer, delineated by its borders from its environment, and its goals were precisely defined. In such a way a system could be "engineered" as shown by Checkland (1999). Such a reductionist simplified approach was insufficient for dealing with the complexity of socio-technical systems, or as it is formulated there, in human affairs. This aspect of SSM has to be underscored when seen from the present perspective of complexity studies – exactly 40 years later.

Soft systems methodology was continuously evolving and included new ideas allowing the study of the complexity of socio-technical systems with more advanced approaches including the role and the perceptions of the observer/participant/researcher. The main features of soft systems methodology are described in detail in Checkland (1999) and in the earlier works. There were several important general components of SSM which were developed in the process of its evolution:

1) The learning process as a foundation of the inquiry, including multiple approaches in defining the system and setting its goals.
2) The seven-stage model of SSM.
3) Four main activities.
4) Customers, actors, transformation, Weltanschauung (world-view), owners, and environmental constraints (CATWOE).
5) Holistic approach.

From the point of view of complexity-related studies the distinction between "hard" and "soft systems" deserves special attention. Referring to the first part of Checkland's book of 1999 it may be concluded that the distinction between "hard" and "soft" systems thinking lies not only in the engineering approach. Well-defined system and external observer, and non-engineering approach vs. fuzzy ill-defined human problems with difficult to define characteristics. The core of the distinction is more profound. It is associated with the definition of the system as determinate ("hard") and indeterminate ("soft"). In the case of the former the world is systemic while in the case of the latter the process of inquiry is systemic.

Looking from the current perspective which also includes knowledge about other interpretations of complexity, it may be concluded that this example of a distinction between "hard" and "soft" systems provides another example of a necessary depth of analysis of the role of observer/participant/analyst expressed in dealing with complexity in management and in project management.

Critical systems thinking and System of Systems Methodologies

Paradoxes associated with the demands of comprehensive holistic understanding what is a system ("everything is related to everything else") led to the development of meta-reflection about the validity of different approaches in understanding the systems and different approaches in systems practice which could be called a "second-order" perspective on systems practice, or critical systems thinking, which has been applied by Jackson (2019) as a framework approach in studying the management of complexity.

The need for critical reflection deriving from the impossibility of fully comprehending any system was for the first time expressed in the 1980s, e.g. Mingers (1980). As Jackson (2019) admits, it also derived from a broader philosophical and social perspective, from Marx through to Habermas and Foucault.

The reflection concerned soft systems thinking in which the different power positions could create equal participation in the studies of social systems. It gave additional impulse for developing reflection on various approaches in systems thinking referring to the ideas of second-order observation – von Foerster (1982), Maturana and Varela (1980), and Luhmann (2012, 2013).

Awareness of critical self-observation of systems theory and systems practice demanded identification of the research area, i.e. the collection of methodological approaches based on systems thinking. Such a set of methodologies was collected by Jackson and Keys (1994) under the name System of Systems Methodologies. As the foundation for ordering this set of ten methodologies, the ideal type grid of problem context was created. Its latest version is depicted in the recent book by Jackson (2019). The grid embodies two dimensions: Systems (complex, complicated, simple) and stakeholders (unitary, pluralist, coercive) and in result nine types of problem were identified.

In the most recent version, the typology of ten systems approaches constituting the System of Systems Methodologies is structured in reference to six types of complexity (Jackson 2019). For simplicity of presentation they are presented in Table 3.2.

Table 3.2 Forms of complexity and types of systems approaches

Type of complexity	*Systems approaches*
Technical complexity	Operational research, systems analysis Systems engineering (Hard systems thinking)
Process complexity	The Vanguard Method (Application and extension of the lean methods)
Structural complexity	System dynamics
Organizational complexity	Socio-technical systems thinking, organizational cybernetics The Viable System Model
People complexity	Strategic Assumption Surfacing and Testing (SAST) Interactive planning Soft systems methodology
Power complexity (Coercive complexity)	Team Syntegrity Critical systems heuristics

Source: Own compilation on the basis of Jackson (2019).

In his discussion on the role of critical systems thinking Jackson (2019) quotes the examples of views expressing the usefulness of a multitude of approaches taken from complexity theory, or complex systems studies, according to terminology applied in this book, in project management (Cooke-Davis 2007; Remington and Pollack 2007). Looking from a current perspective the work of Sheffield *et al.* (2012) can be added.

The multitude of complexity-related approaches deriving from critical systems thinking is a natural source of methods for triangulation in all kinds of research. It is visible in Agile Project Management where, due to necessary adaptiveness, the multitude of methods is somehow natural and essential. It concerns not only the methodologies quoted by Jackson but all methodologies applicable in dealing with complex projects and their environment.

References

Ahern, T., Leavy, B. and Byrne, P.J. (2014) Complex project management as complex problem solving: A distributed knowledge management perspective. *International Journal of Project Management*, Vol. 32, No. 8, pp. 1371–1381. doi: 10.1016/j.ijproman.2013.06.007.

Allen, P., Maguire, S. and McKelvey, B. (eds) (2011), *Handbook of complexity and management*. London: SAGE, pp. 506–523.

American Society for Cybernetics (2003) Regulation and control in human affairs. https://asc-cybernetics.org/foundations/history/prehistory2.htm

Anbari, F.T. (1985) A systems approach to project evaluation. *Project Management Journal*, Vol. 16, No. 3, pp. 21–26.

Anderson, P.C. (1999) Complexity theory and organization science. *Organization Science*, Vol. 10, No. 3, pp. 216–232. doi: 10.1287/orsc.10.3.216.

Ashby, W.R. (1957) *An introduction to cybernetics*. London: Chapman & Hall.

Ashby, W.R. (1958) Requisite variety and its implications for the control of complex systems. *Cybernetica*, Vol. 1, No. 2, pp. 83–99,

Ashby, W. R. (1962). Principles of the self-organizing system, in H. Von Foerster and G. W. Zopf, Jr. (eds), *Principles of self-organization: Transactions of the University of Illinois Symposium*, London: Pergamon Press, pp. 255–278.

Baccarini, D. (1996) The concept of project complexity – A review. *International Journal of Project Management*, Vol. 14, No. 4, pp. 201–204. doi: 10.1016/0263-7863(95)00093-3.

Bakhshi, J., Ireland, V. and Gorod, A. (2016) Clarifying the project complexity construct: Past, present and future. *International Journal of Project Management*, Vol. 34, No. 7, pp. 1199–1213. doi: 10.1016/j.ijproman.2016.06.002.

Bar-Yam, Y. (1997) *Dynamics of complex systems*. Reading, MA: Addison-Wesley.

Bar-Yam, Y. (2003) When systems engineering fails-toward complex systems engineering. In *International conference on systems, man & cybernetics*, Vol. 2, pp. 2021–2028. Piscataway, NJ: IEEE Press. doi: 10.1109/ICSMC.2003.1244709.

Beer, S. (1957) *Cybernetics and management*. Chichester: The English Universities Press Ltd.

Beer, S. (1972) *Brain of the firm*. London: Allen Lane. The Penguin Press.

Beer, S. (1972a) Managing modern complexity. In Landau, R. (ed.), *Complexity, Architectural Design*, October, Vol. XLII, No. 10, pp. 629–632.

Beer, S. (1979) *The heart of the enterprise*. London and New York: John Wiley & Sons.

Beer, S. (1981) *Brain of the firm*, 2nd edition (extended). London and New York: John Wiley & Sons.

Beer, S. (1993) World in torment: A time whose idea must come. *Kybernetes*, Vol. 22, No. 6, pp. 15–43. doi: 10.1108/eb005989.

Beer, S. (1994) *Beyond dispute: The invention of team syntegrity*. New York: John Wiley & Sons.

Biggiero, L. (2001) Sources of complexity. Human systems. *Nonlinear Dynamics, Psychology and Life Sciences*, Vol. 5, No. 1, pp. 3–19. doi: 10.1023/A:1009515211632.

Boisot, M. and McKelvey, B. (2011) Complexity and organization-environment relations: Revisiting Ashby's law of requisite variety. In P. Allen, S. Maguire, , and B. McKelvey (eds), *The SAGE handbook of complexity and management*. Los Angeles: SAGE Publications. Kindle Edition, pp. 279–298.

Boppana, K., Chow, S., de Weck, O.L., LaFon, C., Lekkakos, S.D., Lyneis, J., Rinaldi, M., Wang, Z., Wheeler, P. and Zborovskiy, M. (2008) Can models capture the complexity of the systems engineering process? In A.A. Minai, D. Braha, and Y. Bar-Yam (eds), *Unifying themes in complex systems*. Vol. 6, *Proceedings of the sixth international conference on complex systems*. ISBN 978-3-540-85080-9. Berlin, Heidelberg: Springer-Verlag, pp. 366. doi: 10.1007/978-3-540-85081-6_45.

Botchkarev, A. and Finnigan, P. (2015) Complexity in the context of information systems project management. *Organisational Project Management*, Vol. 2, No. 1, pp. 15–34. doi: 10.5130/opm.v2i1.4272.

Boulding, K.E. (1956) General systems theory: The skeleton of science. *Management Science*, Vol. 2, No. 3, pp. 127–139. doi: 10.1287/mnsc.2.3.197.

Boulton, J.G., Allen, P.M. and Bowman, C. (2015) *Embracing complexity*. Oxford: Oxford University Press.

Brown, S. and Eisenhardt, K. (1998) *Competing on the edge. Strategy as structured chaos*. Cambridge, MA: Harvard Business School Press.

Castellani, B. (2018) Brian Castellani on the complexity sciences. *Art & Science Factory*, 09 February. http://www.art-sciencefactory.com/complexity-map_feb09.html.

Castellani, B. and Hafferty, F.W. (2009) *Sociology and complexity science: A new field of inquiry*. Berlin, Heidelberg: Springer.

Castellani, B. and Gerrits, L.(2021) Map of Complexity Sciences. *Art & Science Factory*. https://www.art-sciencefactory.com/complexity-map_feb09.html.

Casti, J.L. (1994) *Complexification*. New York: Harper Collins.

Checkland, P. (1999) *Systems thinking, systems practice*. Chichester: John Wiley & Sons.

Checkland, P. and Scholes, J. (1990) *Soft systems in action*. New York: John Wiley & Sons.

Chui, G. (2000) Unified theory' is getting closer, Hawking predicts. *San Jose Mercury News*, Morning Final Edition, September 23, pp. 29A.

Cicmil, S., Cooke-Davies, T., Crawford, L. and Richardson, K. (2009) *Exploring the complexity of projects: Implications of complexity theory for project management practice*. Newtown Square, PA: PMI (Kindle edition).

Cilliers, P. (1998) *Complexity and postmodernism*. London and New York: Routledge.

Cleland, D. I. and King, W.R. (1967) *Systems analysis and project management*. New York: McGraw-Hill.

Cleland, D.I. and King, W. R. (1983) *Project management handbook*. New York: Van Nostrand.

Cooke-Davies, T. (2007) *Project management maturity models. The Wiley Guide to Managing Projects*. Hoboken, NJ: John Wiley & Sons. doi: 10.1002/9780470172391.ch49.

Daft, R.L. (1992) *Organization theory and design*, 4th edition. St Paul, MN: West Publishing.

Davis, P.K., McDonald, T., Pendleton-Jullian, A., O'Mahony, A., Osonde, A. and Osoba, A. (2020) *Complex systems agenda for teaching and conducting policy studies*. Santa Monica, CA: RAND Corporation. https://www.rand.org/pubs/working_papers/WR1326.html.

Declaration of Interdependence. https://web.archive.org/web/20180127094805/http://www.pmdoi.org

Drezner, J.A. (2009) *Competition and innovation under complexity*. Santa Monica, CA: RAND Corporation. https://www.rand.org/pubs/reprints/RP1386.html.

Dubberly, H. and Pangaro, P. (2015) Cybernetics and design: Conversations for action. *Cybernetics and Human Knowing*, Vol. 22 (10), pp. 73–82.

Edmonds, B. (2005) What is complexity? - The philosophy of complexity per se with application to some examples in evolution. In F.Heylighen, J. Bollen, and A. Riegler (eds), *The evolution of complexity. The violet book of "Einstein Meets Magritte"*. Dordrecht: Kluwer Academic, pp. 1–16.

Encyclopedia of Complexity and Systems Science. (2009) (ed) Meyers, R.A., New York: Springer Science + Business Media, LLC.

Espejo, R. (2009) Performance management, the nature of regulation and the CyberSyn project. *Kybernetes*, Vol. 38, No. 1–2, pp. 65c82, DOI:10.1108/03684920910930277

Espejo, R. and Harnden, R. (eds) (1989) *The viable system model: Interpretations, and applications of Stafford Beer's VSM*. New York: John Wiley & Sons.

Espinosa, A. and Walker, J. (2017) *A complexity approach to sustainability: Theory and application*. London: World Scientific Press.

Forrester, J.W. (1961) *Industrial Dynamics*. Portland, OR: Productivity Press.

Forrester, J.W. (1971) Counterintuitive Behavior of Social Systems. *Technology Review*, Vol. 73, No. 3, pp. 52–68. DOI: 10.1177/003754977101600202

Forrester, J.W. (1975) *Collected Papers of Jay W. Forrester*. Waltham, MA: Pegasus Communications.

Fuller, R.B. (in collaboration with E.J. Applewhite) (1997) *Synergetics: Explorations in the geometry of thinking*. Online edition hosted by R.W. Gray, originally published by Macmillan, Vol. 1 in 1975 (with a preface and contribution by Arthur L. Loeb; ISBN

0-02-541870-X), Vol. 2 in 1979 (ISBN 0025418807). http://www.rwgrayprojects.com/synergetics/synergetics.html.

Gell-Mann, M. (1994) *The Quark and the Jaguar: Adventures in the simple and the complex*. New York: W.H. Freeman and Company.

Geraldi, J., Maylor, H. and Williams, T. (2011) Now, let's make it really complex (complicated): A systematic review of the complexities of projects. *International Journal of Operations & Production Management*, Vol. 31, No. 9, pp. 966–990. doi:10.1108/01443571111165848.

Geyer F. (1995) The Challenge of Sociocybernetics. *Kybernetes*, Vol. 24, No. 4, pp. 6–32.

Geyer F. and van der Zouwen, J. (1992) Sociocybernetics. in C. V. Negoita (ed), *Handbook of Cybernetics* New York: Marcel Dekker, pp. 95–124.

Gleick, J. (1987) *Chaos: The making of a new science*. New York: Viking Press.

Gleick, J. (2008) *Chaos: Making a new science*. Enhanced Edition, Open Road. Integrated Media. (Kindle edition).

Guide to the Systems Engineering Body of Knowledge (SEBoK) (2021), Stevens Institute, Hoboken, NJ, https://www.sebokwiki.org/w/images/sebokwiki-farmw/2/24/SEBoKv2.5.pdf.

Hall, A.D. (1962) *A methodology for systems engineering*. Princeton, NJ: Van Nostrand.

Heylighen, F. (1999) The growth of structural and functional complexity during evolution. In F. Heylighen, J. Bollen, and A. Riegler (eds), *The evolution of complexity*. Dordrecht: Kluwer Academic, pp. 17–44.

Holland, J.D. (1995) *Hidden order. How adaptation builds complexity*. New York: Basic.

Holland, J.D. (1998) *Emergence: From chaos to order*. Reading, MA: Addison-Wesley.

Holland J. H. (2006) Studying complex adaptive systems. *Journal of Systems Science and Complexity*, Vol. 19, No. 1, pp. 1–8.

Ireland, V. and Statsenko, L. (2020) Managing complex projects and systems: A literature synthesis. *Australian Journal of Multi-Disciplinary Engineering*, Vol. 16, No. 1, pp. 93–110. doi: 10.1080/14488388.2020.1805861.

Jackson, M. and Keys, P. (1984) Towards a system of systems methodologies. *Journal of the Operational Research Society*, Vol. 35, No. 6, pp. 473–486.

Jackson, M.C. (2019) *Critical systems thinking and the management of complexity. Responsible leadership for a complex world*. Hoboken, NJ: John Wiley & Sons.

Kerzner, H. (2009) *Project management: A systems approach to planning, scheduling, and controlling*, Tenth edition. Hoboken, NJ: John Wiley & Sons.

Kerzner, H. (2017) *Project management: A systems approach to planning, scheduling, and controlling*, Twelfth edition. Hoboken, NJ: John Wiley & Sons.

Koestler, A. (1967) *The ghost in the machine*. New York: The Macmillan Company.

Kurtz, C.F. and Snowden, D.J. (2003) The new dynamics of strategy: Sense-making in a complex and complicated world. *IBM Systems Journal*, Vol. 42, No. 3, pp. 462–483.

Li, M. and Vitányi, P. (2008) *An introduction to Kolmogorov complexity and its applications*. New York: Springer.

Lloyd, S. (2001) Measures of complexity: A nonexhaustive list. *IEEE Control Systems Magazine*, Vol. 21, No. 4, pp. 7–8. doi: 10.1109/MCS.2001.939938.

Luhmann, N. (2012) *Theory of society. Vol. I*. Stanford, CA: Stanford University Press.

Luhmann, N. (2013) *Introduction to systems theory*. Cambridge: Polity.

Maturana, H. and Varela, F. (1980) *Autopoiesis and cognition. The realisation of the living*. Boston Studies in the Philosophy of Science # 42. Boston, MA: Riedel Publishing.

Maylor, H., Vidgen, R. and Carver, S. (2008) Managerial complexity in project-based operations: A grounded model and its implications for practice. *Project Management Journal*, Vol. 39, No. 1_suppl. doi: 10.1002/pmj.20057.

Mikkelsen, M. F. (2016) *How to cope with complexity? - A review of project complexity literature using the Cynefin framework as theoretical lens*. Denmark: Novateam. http://www.novateam.dk/PDF/IRIS2016_paper_20.pdf.

Mikkelsen, M. F. (2020) The complex project complexity – Identification of five ideal research types, *The Journal of Modern Project Management*, Vol 7, No 4, https://www.journalmodernpm.com/index.php/jmpm/article/view/JMPM02201.

Mingers, J. (1980) Towards an appropriate social theory for applied systems thinking: Critical theory and soft systems methodology. *Journal of Applied Systems Analysis*, Vol 7, pp. 41–49.

Miser, H.J. and Quade, E.S. (eds) (1985). *Handbook of systems analysis: Overview of uses, procedures, applications, and practice*. New York: North-Holland.

MITRE Systems Engineering Guide (2014) MITRE Corporation. https://www.mitre.org/publications/technical-papers/the-mitre-systems-engineering-guide

Moldoveanu, M. (2004) An intersubjective measure of organizational complexity: A new approach to the study of complexity in organizations. *E:CO*, Vol. 6, No. 3, pp. 9–26.

Moldoveanu, M.C. and Bauer, R.M. (2004) On the relationship between organizational complexity, and organizational structuration. *Organisation Science*, Vol. 15, No. 1, January–February, pp. 98–118. doi:10.1287/orsc.1030.0058.

Navigating Complexity: A Practice Guide (2014) Newtown Square, PA: Project Management Institute.

Pask, G., (1969) The architectural relevance of cybernetics, *Architectural Design*, 7/6, pp. 494–496.

Pask, G. (1975) *The cybernetics of human learning and performance*. London: Hutchinson.

Pask, G. (1975a) *Conversation cognition and learning*. Amsterdam: Elsevier.

Pask, G. (1976) *Conversation theory: Applications in education and epistemology*. Amsterdam: Elsevier.

Pickering, A. (2010) *The cybernetic brain*. Chicago: University of Chicago Press (Kindle edition).

Piney, C. (2008) *Probernetics: The science of successful organizational project management*. Paper presented at PMI® Global Congress 2008—EMEA, St. Julian's, Malta. Newtown Square, PA: Project Management Institute.

Pollack, J. (2007) The changing paradigms of project management. *International Journal of Project Management*, Vol. 25, No. 3, pp. 266–274. doi: 10.1016/j.ijproman.2006.08.002.

Poveda-Bautista, R., Diego-Mas, J.A. and Leon-Medina, D. (2018) Measuring the project management complexity: The case of information technology projects. *Hindawi, Complexity*, Vol. 2018, Article ID 6058480. doi: 10.1155/2018/6058480.

Prigogine, I. and Stengers, I. (1984) *Order out of chaos*. New York: Bantam.

Principia Cybernetica Web. http://pespmc1.vub.ac.be/DEFAULT.html.

Principles behind the Agile Manifesto (2001) http://agilemanifesto.org/principles.html.

Puche-Regaliza, J.C., Jiménez, A. and Arranz-Val, P. (2020) Diagnosis of software projects based on the viable system model. *Systemic Practice and Action Research*, Vol. 33, No. 1, pp. 215–236. doi: 10.1007/s11213-019-09491-y.

Remington, K. and Pollack, J. (2007) *Tools for complex projects*. Gower Publishing, Ltd.

Richardson, K. and Cilliers, P. (2001) Special editors' introduction: What is complexity science? A view from different directions. *Emergence. Complexity and Organization*, Vol. 3, No. 1, pp. 5–23. doi: 10.1207/S15327000EM0301_07.

Scott, B. (2021) *Cybernetics for the social sciences*. Leiden and Boston, MA: Brill.

Shannon, C. E. and Weaver, W. (1949) *The mathematical theory of communication*. Urbana: University of Illinois Press.

Sharrock, E. (2015) *The Agile project manager: Thrive in change with Agile*. Agile Enterprises.

Sheffield, J., Sankaran, S. and Haslett, T. (2012) Systems thinking: Taming complexity in project management. *On the Horizon*, Vol. 20, No. 2, pp. 126 – 136. http://dx.doi.org/10.1108/10748121211235787.

Simon, H.A. (1962) The architecture of complexity. *Proceedings of the American Philosophical Society*, Vol. 106, No. 6, pp. 467–482.

Simon, H.A. (1973) The organization of complex systems. In H. Pattee, (ed) *Hierarchy theory: The challenge of complex systems*. New York: George Braziller, pp. 3–27.

Simon, H.A. (1995) Near decomposability and complexity: How a mind resides in a brain. In J.H. Morowitz and L.J. Singer (eds), *The mind, the brain, and complex adaptive systems*. Reading, MA: Addison-Wesley, pp. 25–44.

Snowden, D. and Goh, Z. (2021) *Cynefin - Weaving sense-making into the fabric of our world*. Singapore: Cognitive Edge Pte Ltd. (Kindle edition).

Stacey, R. (1996) *Strategic management and organisational dynamics. The challenge of complexity*, 2nd edition. London, UK: Pitman Publishing.

Stacey, R.D., Griffin, D. and Shaw, P. (2000) *Complexity and management. Fad or radical challenge to systems thinking*. London and New York: Routledge.

Stacey, R.D. and Mowles, Ch. (2016) *Strategic management and organisational dynamics: The challenge of complexity to ways of thinking about organisations*, 7th edition. Harlow, England: Pearson Education Limited.

Stein, D. L. (1989) *Lectures in the sciences of complexity (Santa Fe Institute Studies in the Sciences of Complexity Lectures)*, 1st Edition, New York: Addison Wesley.

Stevens, S.S. (1946) On the theory of scales of measurement. *Science*, Vol. 103, No. 2684, pp. 677–680. doi: 10.1126/science.103.2684.677.

Trentowski, B.F. (2020) *Stosunek filozofii do cybernetyki (The relation of philosophy to cybernetics, or the art of governing a nation)*, 2nd contemporary edition. Warszawa: Wydawnictwo Naukowe PWN (First edition published in 1843).

Tsoukas, H. and Hatch, M. J. (2001) Complex thinking, complex practice: The case for a narrative approach to organizational complexity. *Human Relations*, Vol. 54, No. 8, pp. 979–1013.

Von Bertalanffy, L. (1968) *General system theory: Foundations, development, applications*. New York: George Braziller.

Von Foerster, H. (1960) On self-organizing systems and their environment, in: *Self-organizing systems*. M.C. Yovits and S. Cameron (eds.), London: Pergamon Press, pp. 31–50.

Von Foerster, H. (1979) Cybernetics of cybernetics. In K. Krippendorff (ed), *Communication and control*. New York: Gordon and Breach, pp. 5–8.

Von Foerster, H. (1982) *Observing systems. A collection of papers by Heinz von Foerster*. Seaside, CA: Inter-Systems Publications.

Von Foerster, H. (2003) *Understanding Understanding: Essays on Cybernetics and Cognition*. New York: Springer.

Von Glasersfeld, E. (1995) *Radical constructivism: A new way of knowing and learning*. London: The Farmer Press.

Waddington, C.H. (1977) *Tools for thought: How to understand and apply the latest scientific techniques of problem solving*. New York: Basic Books.

Waldrop, M.M. (1992) *Complexity: The emerging science at the edge of order and chaos*. New York: Simon & Schuster.

Warfield, J.N. (2006) *An introduction to systems science*. Singapore: World Scientific Publishing Co. Pte. Ltd.

Weaver, W. (1948) Science and complexity. *American Scientist*, Vol. 36, No. 4, pp. 536–544.

Weber, M. (1949) *Methodology of the social sciences*. Glencoe: Free Press.

Whitty, S.J. and Maylor, H. (2009) And then came complex project management (revised). *International Journal of Project Management*, Vol. 27, No. 3, pp. 304–310. doi: 10.1016/J. IJPROMAN.2008.03.004.

Wiener, N. (1948) *Cybernetics: Or control and communication in the animal and the machine*. Pari: Hermann & Cie & Cambridge, MA: MIT Press. 2nd revised ed. 1961.

Wiener, N. (1954) *The human use of human beings: Cybernetics and society*. Boston, MA: Houghton Mifflin.

Williams, T.M. (1999) The need for new paradigms for complex projects. *International Journal of Project Management*, Vol. 17, No. 5, pp. 269–273. doi: 10.1016/S0263-7863(98)00047-7.

Williams, T. (2002) *Modelling complex projects*. Chichester: John Wiley & Sons.

Williams, T. (2005). Assessing and moving on from the dominant project management discourse in the light of project overruns. *IEEE Transactions on Engineering Management*, Vol. 52, No. 4, pp. 497–508.

Wysocki, R. T. (2019). *Effective Project Management. Traditional, Agile, Hybrid, Extreme*, 8th Edition. Indianapolis: John Wiley & Sons.

Yolles, M. (2019) The complexity continuum, part 1: Hard and soft theories. *Kybernetes*, Vol. 48 No. 6, pp. 1330–1354. doi: 10.1108/K-06-2018-0337.

4 Agile project management and complexity science

What is complexity science?

Similarly as in the case of systems thinking, systems approach, and systems theory, significant terminological unclarity accompanies the terms complexity science and complexity theory and constitutes an additional source of misunderstandings in any attempts to systematize the interpretations of complexity. This lack of clarity derives from two streams of interpretations of complexity dominating in scientific discourse since the 1980. The first universal approach embodies all possible usages of the term complexity including purely intuitive meanings and definitions of complexity proposed, for example, by Ashby. The second one, which can be called narrowed, relates the term complexity to a collection of mathematical models developed since the 1970s and embodies such concepts as deterministic chaos, non-equilibrium thermodynamics, synergetics developed by Hermann Haken, catastrophe theory, etc. This approach also is built on analogies and metaphors developed with those mathematical models. The Santa Fe Institute in New Mexico, USA, is perceived as a flagship institution of the second research approach.

The terminological ambiguity concerning complexity science and complexity theory affects both interpretations of complexity, but we focus our attention on the second, narrowed interpretation of complexity. Although in philosophy of science, the term theory has a more specific meaning than science, sometimes those terms are applied with more or less specific clarification when various definitions of complexity are discussed. A selection from the multitude of sources includes the following definitional attempts: Add classics and group them complexity theory (Stacey 2000; Thurner *et al.* 2018; Jackson 2019), complexity theories (Stacey and Mowles 2016), complexity science (Lissack 1999; Richardson and Cilliers 2001), complexity sciences (Castellani 2018; Castellani and Gerrits 2021), or complexity theory and complexity science treated as interchangeable (Stacey and Mowles 2016; Thurner *et al.* 2018). Even more universal interpretations can be found in which complexity and complexity theories are viewed as synonymous (Wells 2013, p. 3). Some authors refer not to complexity theory and/or complexity science but to a new paradigm. In our study we do not extend our research perspective to such a broad scope.

DOI: 10.4324/9781003175032-5

The absence of any significant ordering is also visible in comprehensive monographs concerning studies of complexity in all domains of science (and in similar works in management (Allen *et al.* 2011) where both terms are used interchangeably). It is fully understandable, and our typological proposal of interpretations of complexity and related ideas aims at a preliminary order at least, helpful in further theoretical studies and in the practice of project management and in management.

Following all the above explanations, we use, to some extent arbitrarily, the term complexity science to refer to two universal areas: First, hard complexity science – mathematical models of complexity and complexity-related ideas – and second, soft complexity including analogies and metaphors built with the terms in which those terms are treated as source domains. Following the earlier assumptions, a hybrid approach can be also distinguished. In addition to academic studies on complexity published since the 1980s, this divide also has its roots in the book by Gleick (1987/2008). When quoting Gleick's book it is worthwhile to recall its special significance since it has become the basic reference work for numerous applications of "hard" complexity-related analogies and metaphors in studying "soft" complexity of social systems. Unfortunately, in spite of its very high value, due to its very concept – a popularization book – it had to include some superficial considerations which gave ground to multiple simplifications in further studies of social systems. It must be thus underlined that Gleick's book is an excellent source for developing analogies and metaphors but it can be hardly viewed as a direct source of knowledge about more or less sophisticated mathematical models illustrating complex natural phenomena.

The vocabulary of complexity science includes a large number of terms – intuitive notions, notions taken from other areas of complexity-related studies, and specific indigenous terms either developed to describe mathematical models of complexity or gaining a new meaning within complexity science: Adaptability, adaptation, attractor, bifurcations, butterfly effect, catastrophe, chaos, chaos theory, coevolution, complex adaptive systems, deterministic chaos, dynamical systems, edge of chaos, emerging properties, far-from-equilibrium states, fitness landscape, fractals, learning systems, non-linearity, open system, organized complexity, path dependence, power law, reflexivity, scale-free networks, self-organization, self-organized criticality, self-reflexivity, self-similarity, strange attractor, synergy, synergetics, turbulence, unorganized complexity.

The typology of ideas associated with complexity science is as difficult as the typology of all complexity-related concepts. Therefore the following ordering of descriptions of the ideas associated with complexity science is proposed. The precision of description of each of these ideas is different. It depends on their popularity and significance in project management and in Agile Project Management in particular. The selection may seem arbitrary but it derives from the need for simplification and the aims of our research:

- Chaos theory
- Non-equilibrium thermodynamics

- Complex adaptive systems – mathematical models and qualitative interpretations
- Cellular automata
- Edge of chaos
- Scale-free networks
- Synergetics (Herman Haken)
- Catastrophe theory

Chaos theory

From a perspective of complexity-related studies in the mathematical models called chaos theory should be treated separately because they were predecessors of models labelled complexity theory and/or complexity science.

In a universal the mathematical models called chaos theory refer to dynamical systems reflecting the time dependence of the position of a point in a geometrical space. The state of a dynamical system is depicted with a set of numbers which can be represented as the point in the space. The evolution rule of a dynamical system is represented by the function describing what future states follow the present state. The functions can be deterministic or stochastic.

In 1963, an American climatologist, Lorenz, published his first paper on non-linear dynamical systems in weather forecasting, which remained almost unknown until 1972 when he presented a paper with a provoking metaphor in its title: "Does the Flap of a Butterfly's Wings in Brazil Set off a Tornado in Texas?" (Lorenz 1972).

Chaos models, sometimes called chaos theory, are associated with a specific class of non-linear dynamical systems whose states perceived as random are governed by underlying patterns and deterministic laws that are highly sensitive to initial conditions (Lorenz 1963, 1972/1995). This phenomenon is also called sensitive dependence on initial conditions (SDIC) (Smith 2007) which means that tiny differences in input which can be caused by disturbances, different methods of measurement, or rounding could quickly become overwhelming differences in output. In consequence, any phenomenon described with non-linear models by definition cannot be predicted precisely or is even unpredictable at all. unpredictable precisely, if not predictable at all. They These differences can lead to broadly diverging outcomes making long-term predictions impossible although these systems are deterministic which means that their future evolution follows a unique pattern.

Lorenz had discovered a kind of "chaotic" behaviour of a non-linear system of the weather, but the term chaos was only later given to that phenomenon by the mathematician James A. Yorke (Li and Yorke 1975). An interested aspect of the origins of that term was exposed by Gleick (2008):

> Yorke's paper was important on its merits, but in the end its most influential feature was its mysterious and mischievous title "Period Three Implies

> Chaos". His colleagues advised him to choose something more sober, but Yorke stuck with a word that came to stand for the whole growing business of deterministic disorder.

This incidentally (purposively?) selected name for a mathematical model of "chaos" has brought about an interesting effect in social sciences – multiple uses, misuses, and abuses of analogies and metaphors deriving from the "chaos theory". The cases of "catchy" terms of "chaos" and the "butterfly effect" show that sometimes the name given to an abstract mathematical model can stir additional, sometimes too superficial attention in studying broadly defined social phenomena. It is an important factor in studying the links between complexity-related ideas and fuzzily defined notions associated with Agile Project Management.

The term "chaos" is associated with a specific type of dynamical system which formalizes deterministic unpredictability without considering any probabilistic element. Origins of studies of this type of dynamical systems are rooted in the works of Poincaré on the three-body problem in physics published at the end of the 19th century and the beginning of the 20th century (Bishop 2017). In the meantime there were also studies dealing with dynamical systems published by other authors, yet the properties of dynamical systems were not studied until the early 1960s when a climatologist Lorenz published his works.

When discussing chaos models and their direct applications as well as their role as the source domain for analogies and metaphors in social studies, an additional comment concerning non-linearity is necessary. In many cases in the applications of complexity-related ideas in the studies of social systems non-linearity is presented as a kind of extraordinary property. To avoid this misunderstanding it's worthwhile to quote Stan Ulam who commented on the extraordinary attention given to the non-linearity of mathematical systems and natural phenomena. "Stan once remarked that this was 'like defining the bulk of zoology by calling it the study of non-elephant animals'" (Campbell 1987, p. 218).

There is a rank of characteristics of mathematical models of the deterministic chaos. The most common ones, which have become the sources of various metaphors associated with chaos models are fractal, strange attractor, and bifurcation.

Specific self-similar, recursive geometrical structures with non-integer dimensions. Such structures were earlier known in mathematics, e.g. the Koch Snowflake or Sierpiński Carpet. Their properties were discovered by Benoit Mandelbrot (1982) who called them fractals to reflect their specific dimensionality.

In the theory of dynamical systems an attractor is a set of states in the state space, or more specifically in the phase space, towards which the system tends to evolve from a broad variety of initial conditions. When a system is in the state close to the attractor, a small disturbance cannot remove it from that state.

An attractor can be a point, a set of points, a curve, a manifold. In the chaos models the key element is the so-called strange attractor which has a fractal structure.

An important property of chaos theory has to be taken into account when applied in studying social systems. It was put forward by Cilliers (1998, p. 9):

> When analysing complex systems, a sensitivity to initial conditions, for example, is not such an important issue. As a matter of fact, it is exactly the robust nature of complex systems, i.e. their capability to perform in the same way under different conditions, that ensures their survival. Although the metaphor of the butterfly's flapping wings causing a tornado on the other side of the globe is a good one for describing a sensitivity to initial conditions, it has caused so much confusion.

Synergetics of Hermann Haken

Synergy, a phenomenon occurring in physical, chemical, biological, and social systems, belongs also to the fundamental concepts of modern management. In a dominating but simplified interpretation, not-too-correctly assigned to Aristotle (Cohen 2020), synergy is treated as a surplus, an effect of interactions of multiple elements, illustrated with the metaphoric equation 2 + 2 = 5. It has become one of the most popular "buzzwords" of modern management. A deepened analysis of the meaning of synergy shows that the surplus effect constitutes only one example of its occurrence.

According to the Online Etymology Dictionary, the term synergy meaning cooperation derives from Modern Latin *synergia*, from Greek *synergia* "joint work, a working together, cooperation; assistance, help", from *synergos* "working together", related to *synergein* "work together, help another in work", from *syn-* "together" (see syn-) + *ergon* "work".

Synergy as a philosophical concept and as an attribute of collective phenomena in nature and society has been known since antiquity. Its rigorous study began in the 19th century. It also has attracted attention in various areas of systems studies. The role of synergy in nature, in human development, and its relations with complex systems were objects of thorough research by Corning (2003) who defined synergy as: "combined, or cooperative, effects produced by the relationships among various forces, particles, elements, parts, or individuals in a given context – effects that are not otherwise possible" and identified, among others, the following varieties of synergy: Synergies of scale, threshold effects, phase transition, synergy as an emerging phenomenon, combination of labour. It must be also underscored that synergy can be also negative, i.e. when the effects of interactions diminish the final effect (Corning 2003).

The meaning of synergy in management is usually associated with the surplus resulting from cooperation. Ansoff (1965, 1987) who studied the role of synergy in strategic management also took into account the possibility of negative synergy. It is also an important element of the management cybernetics of Stafford Beer – syntegrity and syntegration, already mentioned (Beer 1994). Achieving synergies in finance, innovation, and manufacturing constitutes the main objective of mergers and acquisitions.

Used in a general sense, synergy as an attribute of project management was referred to in multiple works, usually treated as an element of professional knowledge.

Since the very onset of Agile Project Management, synergy was regarded as an important attribute of the project teams contributing to their effectiveness, e.g. in the ASD (Highsmith 2000), DSDM (Highsmith 2002, p. 139). The applications of various interpretations of synergy in Agile Project Management will be dealt with in detail in later parts of the book.

Synergy can be frequently found in the names of companies, especially management consulting ones, including software development. Those companies, by using this term as their firm name, try to underscore their high competences in helping customers in achieving their management goals in the most effective way. It is also reflected in a simple slogan: TEAM – Together Everyone Achieves More.

There are two comprehensive proposals of theoretical concepts and practical applications whose authors used the term synergetics. They are presented here according to the order of the proposed typology of interpretations of complexity. The first, developed by Hermann Haken, is included in complexity science (Stacey 2000). The second, an indigenous and partly forgotten comprehensive multi- and inter-disciplinary "Grand Vision" invented and propagated by R. Buckminster Fuller (1979), is treated as the source of indigenous complexity-related ideas and discussed in a subsequent part of the book.

It should be added that in these two examples of studying the ideas associated with variously defined synergy, theoretical considerations and applications were given scientific meaning by adding -ics. In the Online Etymology Dictionary:

> -ics in the names of sciences or disciplines (acoustics, aerobics, economics, etc.). revival of the classical custom of using the neuter plural of adjectives with Greek -ikos "pertaining to" (see -ic) to mean "matters relevant to" and also as the titles of treatises about them.

Synergetics in a version proposed by Hermann Haken is described in numerous works of its author, his co-researchers, and followers (Haken 1983; Pelster and Wunner 2016), and in the Synergetics Series from Springer including about 80 books. Therefore only a brief introductory survey of its main characteristics and its applications in management and in project management is presented.

The term Synergetik (in German) as the science of cooperation was used for the first time in (Haken and Graham 1971). The direct inspiration for developing synergetics derived from laser theory (Haken 1983). Although it was originally initiated as the study of non-equilibrium phase transition in physics, chemistry, and biology, the proposed ideas were regarded as relevant not only to laser theory but also to economics, psychology, sociology, linguistics, cognitive science, and in other areas.

According to a universal interpretation proposed by Haken (2016, p. 150), synergetics deals with systems composed of many parts or elements and distinguishes between the macroscopic level and the microscopic level by length- and/or time-scale separation. Synergetics studies the spontaneous formation of temporal, spatial, and functional structures, i.e. the emergence of new qualities via self-organization in open systems. The main aim of synergetics is to disclose the principles (or laws) underlying self-organization irrespective of the nature of the individual parts of the considered systems. Synergetics in its mature form, treated as inter-disciplinary science, is focused on material or immaterial systems, composed of many individual parts such as atoms, photons, molecules, neurons, and people in society.

The examples of direct applications of synergetics in management-related areas include (Haken 2007):

- Sociology: Dynamics of groups, collective formation of order parameters governing human behaviour including the formation of public opinion, etc.
- The economy: e.g. Schumpeter cycle, competition between companies, synergy effects
- Philosophy: The concept of self-organization, strong vs. weak emergence
- Epistemology: The establishment of paradigms in the sense of Thomas S. Kuhn
- Control theory: Indirect control via control parameters
- Information theory: Compression and inflation of information, change of information in self-organization processes
- Management theory: Indirect control of processes, corporate identity, "social climate", etc., as order parameters

The concepts of Ralph Stacey and the Cynefin Framework by Dave Snowden

The ideas of Ralph Stacey and the Cynefin Framework developed by Dave Snowden and rooted in complexity science, since the turn of the 20th century, have exerted an immense impact on management and project management, including Agile Project Management. They are to some extent similar, in the most general sense. They both partly derive from complexity science-related models, analogies, and metaphors although with differing interpretations of the same notions, predominantly complexity and chaos.

Complexity of organization by Ralph Stacey

The studies of relations between various complexity science-related concepts and management, predominantly strategic management, gradually developed by Ralph Stacey since the early 1990s constitute one of the key contributions shaping the ways of thinking about complexity in managing organizations. In his books (Stacey 1993, 1996, 1996a, 2000) and together with his co-authors (Stacey *et al.* 2000; Stacey and Mowles 2016), Stacey has revealed how chaos theory, dissipative structures, synergetics, cybernetics, systems theory, and complex adaptive systems could shape the modern universal theory of management and theoretical foundations of innovativeness, organization dynamics, knowledge management, and learning in management. It is also necessary to underscore an evolution in the ideas of Stacey. His interpretations of chaos and complexity from the earlier works, e.g. Stacey (1993, 1996), are different from the interpretations from the later works e.g. (Stacey 2000; Stacey *et al.* 2000; Stacey and Mowles 2016). The main value of the ideas developed by Stacey is their scope and depth, beginning from philosophical reflections through detailed proposals of applications of complexity science-related ideas in management and ending with the analysis of psychological and psychoanalytical factors shaping organization and determining its complexity.

From the rich collection of ideas of Stacey and his co-researchers, three topics are of special importance:

1. The theoretical concept of organization and its complexity.
2. Applications of complexity-related ideas as analogies and metaphors in the theory and practice of management.
3. A comprehensive theoretical scheme which under the name Stacey Matrix has become one of most influential concepts in management theory and practice, paradoxically in collision with the initial intentions of the author.

Focusing on organization we have to consider the following problems. How do we define the complexity of an organization? To what extent can the knowledge about the complexity of natural systems – physical, chemical, biological – be helpful in developing a more cognitively valuable and better understanding of an organization? How can we understand the interactions between actors, members of organization who at the same time create the organization?

In classical approaches to complexity described in Chapter 3, the complexity of social systems could be interpreted with mathematical models, analogies, and metaphors drawn from the natural sciences. The degree of reflexivity of the participant-observer could be different, from the pure independence of a mathematical modeller to the various levels of self-observation of the participant-observer. The consequences of the role of the observer are the key problem in philosophy of social sciences and are often scrutinized in the works on complexity and management. Stacey and his team have innovative answers to the above questions.

They are included in understanding organizations as complex responsive processes of relating (later referred to as CRPR). This idea has been presented in several works of Stacey and his co-workers. It is described here in an introductory way with reference to (Stacey 2000) and (Stacey *et al.* 2000).

A new approach to organizations aiming at explaining their complexity in a more profound manner has its roots in psychology, psychoanalysis, communication theory, and social constructionism. Relationship psychology is used as a foundation of a new understanding of organizations.

From the perspective of an individual-centred psychology, the analogue of a complex adaptive system in human terms is a group of individuals treated as agents. Self-organization is understood as individuals organizing themselves in a group/team. The manager is treated as a kind of external programmer setting the rules of behaviour of the team members to achieve desired goals by organizing themselves. The perspective of relationship psychology provides other insights. When the analogy with complex adaptive systems is used then the analogue of agents is the themes organizing conversations, communication, and power relations. In such interpretations it is not the individuals who organize themselves but the pattern of their relationships in communicational and power terms. The process of communicating is an analogue of a complex adaptive system (Stacey 2000, p. 148). Self-organization occurs in the processes of collective communication, i.e. in conversations.

This interpretation leads to the conclusion that human systems are not systems in which the agents adapt to each other according to their mental models. Humans make gestures that evoke and provoke responses from each other. Therefore the word "adaptive" has to be replaced with the word "responsive". Human interactions are interpreted too mechanistically; thus, instead, it's more adequate to reality to conclude that human relating is made up of complex responsive processes (Stacey 2000, p. 148).

The above description shows the depth of understanding of organizations. The key novelty of the proposed new interpretation of complexity of organizations is included in the following declaration (Stacey *et al.* 2000, p. 188):

> The move we want to make … is away from thinking about an organization as a system, to thinking about organizing as highly complex ongoing process of people relating to each other. We refer to this as the Complex Responsive Processes of Relating. In this understanding of systems it is not possible to treat them as an equivalent of engineering system. Systems are tools of communication, ways of talking, similar to any other in an organization, with the important difference that they are formalized and provide legitimation for talk and other action.

A novelty of this approach is based on reference to relationship psychology (Stacey 2000). In a more general ontological, epistemological, and epistemological context, Stacey and his co-workers Stacey *et al.* (2000), go a step further by analysing complex human organizations from a teleological point of view. These considerations lead to the crucial problem. How can ideas of complexity borrowed from non-social areas of knowledge be used in understanding organization and its complexity, or in a broader sense, all kinds of human systems?

The introductory answer of Stacey and co-researchers (Stacey *et al.* 2000, p. 191) is relatively simple but demands further elucidation. They conclude that complexity sciences understood as a collection of mathematical and simulation models are a source domain from which it is possible to derive insights about human interaction by way of analogy. However, they do not propose to use complexity sciences as a source of loose metaphor because it could lead to yet another management fad.

This declaration is very resolute. When taken consistently we will have to agree that all attempts to model organization as a complex adaptive system are incorrect since the analogy lies deeper. A complex adaptive system is an analogy for communicating systems and not for a system of interactions of actors, members of the system. By using this argument the Stacey's team prove that the classical understanding of the transfer by analogies and metaphors from complexity science to human systems is not valuable epistemologically. The decisive role for the validity of such transfer is played by the mathematical models. They repeat the argument of McKelvey (1999) that a complexity theory of organization built solely on analogies and metaphors could become just a fad as defined in management theory and practice (Newell *et al.* 2001).

Bearing in mind this conclusion about the fad character of applications of complexity-related ideas in management, Stacey and co-workers make an observation that the transfer of knowledge with the use of analogies is more useful than the transfer of knowledge by metaphors. The concept transferred analogically must be better understood in the source domain and there must be a more precise morphism of the ideas between the source field and the target field. However, following McKelvey (1999), they observe that the validity of such transfers is fundamentally insufficient because of the limited predictability treated as the key function of theory, even in the post-positivist world. Their main conclusion about the transfer of knowledge from complexity science to management and about the validity of the idea of complex responsive processes of relating can be expressed as follows (Stacey *et al.* 2000, p. 204). "We think that management practice does not change through specific actionable proposals but through the evolving ways of thinking and talking of groupings of managers that produce emergent action".

The above short introduction to the research of Stacey and co-researchers on the role of complexity-related ideas in management theory and practice is to some extent simplified but seems to be sufficient for our research purposes. More extended and profound studies of the role of complex responsive processes of relating and similar ideas in management are included in a recent book by Stacey and Mowley (2016). The following of conclusions stemming from the above discussion must be borne in mind in all discussions on the impact of complexity-related ideas applied in Agile Project Management frameworks:

1. The concept of complex responsive processes of relating shows the profundity and at the same time limits of applications of ideas from complexity

studies of natural systems in studying organization at the micro-level in which direct communication plays a decisive role.

2. These radical arguments cannot be treated as support for a complete rejection of the use of analogies and metaphors deriving from various strands of complexity-related studies of natural systems. They only include an appeal for cautiousness in applying such analogies and metaphors and awareness of their limitations.
3. It must be remembered, and it is omitted in all considerations on the role of mathematical modelling in defining complex responsive processes of relating, that operationalization can be based on multiple simplifying assumptions (border conditions) in which the modellers operationalize qualitative (observer-dependent) characteristics. Therefore making mathematical modelling the ultimate argument determining the value of applications of complexity-based ideas in studying organizations may seem to be too radical.
4. Taking into account that the applications of complexity-related ideas in Agile Project Management are predominantly built on analogies and metaphors, the concept of CRPR can be seen as a certain road sign for deeper studies and the source of cautiousness in using those analogies and metaphors.

In addition to the doubts concerning complete resignation from applications of analogies and metaphors based on the complexity of natural phenomena in organization theory and practice, a few remarks concerning the idea of complex responsive processes of relating must be presented. CRPR is built on interpersonal conversation and communication which constitute the key determinants of creating organization. However, it has to be remembered that similar ideas had been developed earlier, of course without the present knowledge of complexity and Stacey's depth of analysis. Conversation was the central element of the already mentioned concept of cybernetics developed by Gordon Pask (1975, 1975a). Additionally, when studying the role of interpersonal communication in creating organizations it seems necessary to mention the idea of a social system defined as a system of meaningful communication proposed by Niklas Luhmann (1996).

Both Stacey's ideas on the role of complexity science in management presented in the first phase of his studies and complex responsive processes promulgated in the second phase have made an important contribution to management theory and practice. However, the most popular concept of Stacey's remains the diagram commonly known as the "Stacey Matrix". The "Stacey Matrix" distinguishes degrees of simplicity, complication, complexity, and chaos along two dimensions: (X) degree of certainty of changes affecting managers and members of the organization, and (Y) degree of agreement between managers and members of the organization under the conditions of anxiety deriving from uncertainty. It was published for the first time in the 2nd edition of his fundamental monograph (Stacey 1996, p. 47). It was removed from the 3rd edition (Stacey 2000).

The reasons for abandoning the diagram were explained by Stacey in a comment to a paper on the role of coaching in dealing with complexity (Stacey 2012, pp. 92–93). According to the initial intentions of the author, the diagram was designed as a device for classifying different decision-making and control procedures presented in the management literature in reference to the assumptions about their context. The diagram illustrated the relations between those procedures. The purpose was to understand more clearly the nature of different prescriptions researchers had made. Surprisingly, as Stacey observes, the diagram took on a life of its own and began to be used as a description of contingency theory which managers could use to rationally identify the context and then choose the most appropriate procedure. Adding to this a critical approach to the special role of managers as objective observers in complex organizations (Stacey 2000, pp. 310–311; Stacey *et al.* 2000, pp. 205–206) Stacey's decision seems justified.

The life of the diagram continues. Sometime in its original form or in a changed interpretation it can be still frequently found in complexity-related works in management and in project management. It remains very popular among consulting companies and practitioners. A special version of the Stacey Matrix is regarded as a part of the theory and practice of complexity in Agile Project Management by the Project Management Institute. It has a very specific name reflecting the critical approach of its author – see Figure 4.1.

A question arises of whether it is necessary to abandon the various interpretations of the Stacey Matrix in its "new life". Using a more advanced,

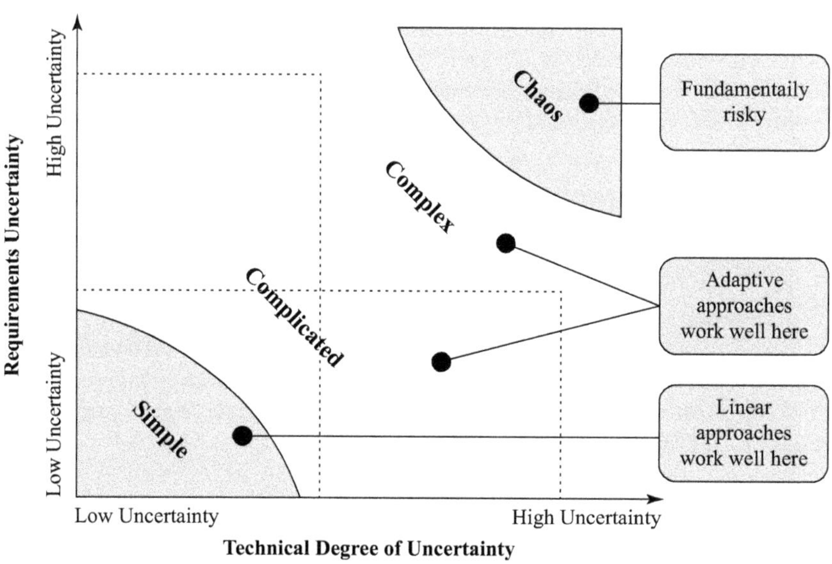

Figure 4.1 Uncertainty and complexity model inspired by the Stacey Complexity Model. Source: *Agile Practice Guide* (2017).

constructivist approach, also referring to the role of conversation and negotiated meaning, the following interpretation can be found. In the discourse between the author and the audience, a large part of the latter has discovered a more dominant meaning of the diagram. It reflects the deepest intuitive understanding of relations between the meaning of commonly applied terms: Simple (known), complicated (partially known but reduced to the known), complex (partially known and partially not-known), and chaotic (unknown and unknowable). If this simplified interpretation stimulated a proper understanding and actions thus it can be applied and proliferated. In the case of more advanced applications, as for example, in Agile Project Management, the knowledge about a deeper meaning understanding of the diagram would be necessary.

The examples of applications of the Stacey's and his co-researchers' ideas in project management, including the Agile methodological frameworks, reflect the triadic divide of their research area.

The first group is made up of the references to complexity not relating to the Stacey's diagram. As the examples the following works can be quoted: (Remington and Pollack 2007; Geraldi *et al.* 2011).

In the second group, references to the Stacey Matrix are most frequent and the examples are just selected randomly. As influential examples, Schwaber and Beedle (2002, p. 93) and Schwaber (2004, p. 5; 2009, p. 26) can be recalled. It will be given more attention in the part devoted to the origins of Scrum – Chapter 6.

The applications of complex responsive processes of relating in project management are not frequent yet. As an example of a comprehensive application of CRPR in project management the book by Cicmil *et al.* (2009) can be recalled. The book (Stacey *et al.* 2000) has been also mentioned in *Navigating Complexity* (2014) but without any direct reference to the CRPR.

Cynefin

Cynefin, in Welsh equivalent to home, habitat, the German Heimat, or, as recently interpreted, "Place of Your Multiple Belongings" (Snowden and Goh 2021, p. 17), is another comprehensive collection of complexity-related ideas applied in various areas of management theory and practice, in policy making, governance, security, etc. It was developed by Dave Snowden in the late 1990s and in the beginning of the 21st century (Kurtz and Snowden 2003).

Looking from the point of view of the divide between "hard" and "soft" complexity, the authors of Cynefin represent a specific point of view. In other typical hybrid interpretations, the authors make attempts to operationalize and build simulation models of their ideas, at least partly. In Cynefin, the proposed approach is different. Cynefin is considered as a sense-making framework, which means that its value is not so much in logical arguments or empirical verifications as in its effect on the sense-making and decision-making capabilities of those who use it. Kurtz and Snowden (2003) proposed to extend simulations with metaphors (complexity, chaos, and order) rooted in the vocabulary of myths and stories drawn from different ancient civilizations. A very inspiring metaphor was once applied by Kurtz and Snowden (2008) to describe organization and its complexity: "Bramble bushes in a thicket".

The Cynefin Framework gradually evolved in the subsequent works of its author and co-workers. One of its versions was illustrated in an impactful paper of Snowden and Boone (2007) exposing the usefulness of Cynefin in the managerial decision-making process. The evolution of Cynefin is presented in detail in the recently published book (Snowden and Goh 2021). According to its founder, in its present interpretation (Snowden and Goh 2021, p. 76):

> Cynefin is a key framework in what is known as Naturalizing sense-making. The term naturalizing relates to the use of natural science, and sense-making (with a hyphen) is defined as, "How do we make sense of the world so that we can act in it?" Cynefin is also part of a body of work looking at the dynamic interplay between deductive, inductive, and abductive sense-making.

The most recent version of the Cynefin Framework constituting a synthesis of its evolution was published in February 2021 – see Figure 4.2.

This version is explained in detail on the websites run by Cynefin Team on Cynefin Wiki and the Cognitive Edge. In the most recent short version the

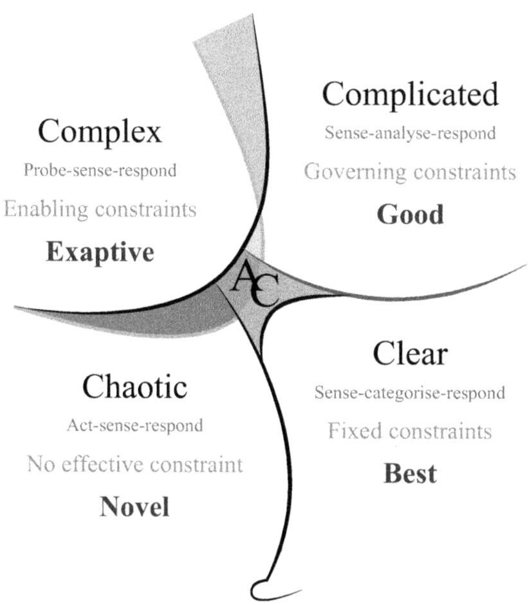

Figure 4.2 Recent version of Cynefin. Source: Cynefin (2021).

primary definition of Cynefin is, at its heart, about a flow of engagement over time with things known, unknown, and unknowable, loved, and unloved all, which entangle our lives and create meaning (Snowden and Goh 2021, p. 52).

To help to refine the uses of complexity-related ideas in Agile Project Management and in general, in project management, it's worthwhile to refer directly to recently published errors of interpretations of Cynefin enumerated by Snowden on his blog (Snowden 2021):

- Using Cynefin as a two-by-two matrix for rigid categorization.
- Thinking that Cynefin and the Stacey Matrix are the same thing.
- Assuming the linear experiments work in the complex domain – i.e. not understanding the need for parallel probes around a coherent hypothesis.
- Talking about the five quadrants of Cynefin.
- Confusing chaos with disorder (now aporetic), chaos is the absence of effective constraints while the aporetic is a state of unknowing, there may be possible constraints.
- Confusing chaos with complexity – traffic in Indian cities is complex, not chaotic in the main.
- Failing to realise that chaos is always a temporary state.
- Arguing Cynefin uses the word chaos incorrectly – it's a new field and there is no agreement on the term. People into deterministic chaos get excited about this, but the word is used differently in different disciplines.
- Assuming that Cynefin is complexity theory, or is only about complexity – it isn't, it uses it but it's not the only theory base behind Cynefin.
- Thinking that the only response to chaos in Cynefin is to exit quickly; it isn't, as entering deliberately (the liminal domain) is key to decision making under conditions of uncertainty.
- The Cynefin Framework occupies an important place in Agile Project Management. Snowden underscored the mutual relations between Cynefin and Agile Project Management by exposing his own role in founding the DSDM and in supporting the development of Extreme Programming (XP). He also stressed that the Agile Manifesto and Cynefin are the same age and although they evolved separately, at present they are closely connected (Snowden and Goh 2021, p. 68).

An interesting observation concerning Cynefin, Scrum, and the Stacey Matrix was made by Snowden in the anniversary book:

> Scrum (the dominant method within the Agile movement) had in part grown up around the Stacey Matrix, which uses some of the same language, but is different in nature. Cynefin is about how things are, how we know them and how we perceive them, while Stacey focuses more on perception.
>
> (Snowden and Goh 2021, p. 68)

The impact of Cynefin on applications of complexity-related ideas in project management, including the Agile methodological frameworks, can be illustrated with scores of examples. In the case of non-Agile project management, the most influential in the literature is the series of publications by Mikkelsen.

Summary

Although the concepts of Stacey and his team and the Cynefin Framework are to some extent different, they both have found their stable place in the development of project management theory including Agile Project Management. Their main common denominator is the attempts to deepen the intuitive interpretations of complexity-related ideas in management. The above shortened descriptions follow the aim of this book. When applying these concepts, it is necessary to go to the roots of the ideas. It also must be remembered that they have changed and they are still changing. We hope that the ideas of Ralph Stacey, who passed away in September 2021, in the time when we were writing this book, will be developed by his disciples and followers.

References

Agile Practice Guide (2017) Newtown Square, PA: Project Management Institute.

Allen, P., Maguire, S. and McKelvey, B. (eds) (2011) *The Sage handbook of complexity and management*. Los Angeles, CA: SAGE.

Ansoff, H.I. (1965) *Corporate strategy – An analytic approach to business policy for growth and expansion*. New York: McGraw-Hill.

Ansoff, H.I. (1987) *Corporate strategy*. Harmondsworth, UK: Penguin.

Beer, S. (1994) *Beyond dispute: The invention of team syntegrity*. New York: Wiley.

Bennis, W. and Biederman, P. (1997) *Organizing genius: The secrets of creative collaboration*. Reading, MA and New York: Addison-Wesley Publishing Co.

Bishop, R. (2017) *"Chaos", The Stanford encyclopedia of philosophy* (Spring 2017 edition). Edward N. Zalta (ed.). https://plato.stanford.edu/archives/spr2017/entries/chaos.

Buckminster Fuller Institute. San Francisco, https://www.bfi.org/.

Campbell, D. K. (1987) Nonlinear science from paradigms to practicalities. *Los Alamos Science Special Issue*, No. 15, pp. 218–262.

Castellani, B. (2018) Brian Castellani on the complexity sciences. *Art & Science Factory*, 09 February. http://www.art-sciencefactory.com/complexity-map_feb09.html.

Castellani, B. and Gerrits, L. (2021) Map of Complexity Sciences. *Art & Science Factory*. https://www.art-sciencefactory.com /complexity-map feb09.html.

Cicmil, S., Cooke-Davies, T., Crawford, L. and Richardson, K. (2009) *Exploring the complexity of projects: Implications of complexity theory for project management practice*. Newtown Square, PA: PMI (Kindle edition).

Cilliers, P. (1998) *Complexity and postmodernism*. London and New York: Routledge.

Cohen, S. M. (2020) "Aristotle's Metaphysics", *The Stanford Encyclopedia of Philosophy (Fall 2020 Edition)*, E. N. Zalta (ed.). https://plato.stanford.edu/archives/fall2020/entries/aristotle-metaphysics/

Corning, P.A. (2003) *Nature's magic: Synergy in evolution and the fate of humankind*. Cambridge: Cambridge University Press (Kindle edition).

Cynefin (2021) https://cynefin.io/wiki/Cynefin.

Fuller, R.B. (in collaboration with E.J. Applewhite) (1997) *Synergetics: Explorations in the geometry of thinking*. Online edition hosted by R.W. Gray, originally published by Macmillan, Vol. 1 in 1975 (with a preface and contribution by Arthur L. Loeb; ISBN 0-02-541870-X), vol. 2 in 1979 (ISBN 0025418807). http://www.rwgrayprojects.com /synergetics/synergetics.html.

Geraldi, J., Maylor, H. and Williams, T. (2011) Now, let's make it really complex (complicated): A systematic review of the complexities of projects. *International Journal of Operations & Production Management*, Vol. 31, No. 9, pp. 966–990. doi:10.1108/01443571111165848.

Gleick, J. (1987) *Chaos: The making of a new science*. New York: Viking Press.

Gleick, J. (2008) *Chaos: Making a new science*. Enhanced Edition, New York: Open Road. Integrated Media (Kindle edition).

Haken, H. (1983) *Synergetics. An introduction nonequilibrium phase transitions and self-organization in physics, chemistry, and biology*. Berlin, Heidelberg, New York, and Tokyo: Third Revised and Enlarged Edition, Springer-Verlag.

Haken, H. (2007) Synergetics. *Scholarpedia*, Vol. 2, No. 1, pp. 1400, http://www .scholarpedia.org/article/Synergetics. doi: 10.4249/scholarpedia.1400.

Haken, H. (2016) The brain as a synergetic and physical system. In A. Pelster and G.Wunner (eds), *Selforganization in complex systems: The past, present, and future of synergetics. Proceedings of the international symposium*. Hanse Institute of Advanced Studies, Delmenhorst, Germany, November 13–16, 2012, Switzerland: Springer International, pp. 147–164.

Haken, H. and Graham, R. (1971) Synergetik - die Lehre vom Zusammenwirken. *Umschau*, Vol. 6, pp. 191–195.

Highsmith, J.A. III (2000) *Adaptive software development. A collaborative approach to managing complex systems*. New York: Dorset House Publishing Co. (Kindle edition).

Highsmith, J. (2002). *Agile Software Development Ecosystems*. Boston: Addison-Wesley.

Jackson, M.C. (2019) *Critical systems thinking and the management of complexity. Responsible leadership for a complex world*. Hoboken, NJ: John Wiley & Sons.

Kurtz, C.F. and Snowden, D.J. (2003) The new dynamics of strategy: Sense-making in a complex and complicated world. *IBM Systems Journal*, Vol. 42, No. 3, pp. 462–483.

Kurtz, C.F. and Snowden, D. J. (2008). Bramble bushes in a thicket: Narrative and the intangibles of learning networks, in M. Gibbert and T. Durand (eds), *Strategic Networks: learning to compete*, Oxford: Blackwell, pp. 121–50.

Li, T.-Y., and Yorke, J.A. (1975) Period three implies chaos. *The American Mathematical Monthly*, Vol. 82, No. 10, pp. 985–992.

Lissack, M.R. (1999) Complexity: The science, its vocabulary, and its relation to organizations. *Emergence*, Vol. 1, No. 1, pp. 110–126. doi: 10.1207/s15327000em0101_7.

Lorenz, E.N. (1963) Deterministic non periodic flow. *Journal of the Atmospheric Sciences*, Vol. 20, pp. 130–141. doi: 10.1175/1520-0469(1963)020<0130:DNF>2.0.CO;2.

Lorenz, E.N. (1972) Predictability: Does the flap of a butterfly's wings in Brazil set off a tornado in Texas? In *139th annual meeting of the American Association for the Advancement of Science* (29 December 1972), in *Essence of Chaos* (1995), Appendix 1, 181.

Luhmann, N. (1996) *Social systems*. Translated by John Bednarz, Jr. with Dirk Baecker. Stanford, CA: Stanford University Press.

Mandelbrot, B.B. (1982) *The fractal geometry of nature*. New York: W. H. Freeman and Co.

McKelvey, B. (1999) Complexity theory in organization science: Seizing the promise or becoming a fad? *Emergence*, Vol. 1, No. 1, pp. 5–32. doi: 10.1207/S15327000EM0101_2.

Merriam-Webster Dictionary (2019) https://www.merriam-webster.com/dictionary/.

Newell, S., Robertson, M. and Swan, J. (2001) Management fads and fashions. *Organization*, Vol. 8, No. 1, pp. 5–15. doi: 10.1177/135050840181001.

Online Etymology Dictionary, https://www.etymonline.com.

Pelster, A. and Wunner, G. (eds) (2016) Selforganization in complex systems: The past, present, and future of synergetics. In *Proceedings of the international symposium*. Hanse Institute of Advanced Studies, Delmenhorst, Germany, November 13–16, 2012, Switzerland: Springer International, Publishing AG.

Remington, K. and Pollack, J. (2007) *Tools for complex projects*. Aldershot: Gower Publishing, Ltd.

Richardson, K. and Cilliers, P. (2001) Special editors' introduction: What is complexity science? A view from different directions. *Emergence*. Complexity and Organization, Vol. 3, No. 1, pp. 5–23. doi: 10.1207/S15327000EM0301_07.

Schwaber, K. (2004) *Agile project management with Scrum*. Redmond, WA: Microsoft Press.

Schwaber, K. (2009) *Agile project management with Scrum*. Redmond, WA: Microsoft Press.

Schwaber, K. and Beedle, M. (foreword by Jeff Sutherland) (2002) *Agile software development with Scrum*. Upper Saddle River, NJ: Prentice Hall.

Smith, L.A. (2007) *Chaos: A very short introduction*. Oxford: Oxford University Press.

Snowden, D. (2021) *Common errors in talking about and using Cynefin*, https://www.cognitive-edge.com/cynefin-st-davids-2021-3-of-3/

Snowden, D. and Goh, Z. (2021) *Cynefin - weaving sense-making into the fabric of our world*. Singapore: Cognitive Edge Pte Ltd. (Kindle edition).

Snowden, D.J. and Boone, M.E. (2007) A leader's framework for decision making. *Harvard Business Review*, November, Vol. 85, No. 11, pp. 68–76.

Stacey, R. (1993) *Strategic management and organisational dynamics*. London, UK: Pitman Publishing.

Stacey, R. (1996) *Strategic management and organisational dynamics*. The Challenge of Complexity, 2nd edition. London, UK: Pitman Publishing.

Stacey, R.D. (1996a) *Complexity and creativity in organizations*. San Francisco, CA: Berrett-Koehler.

Stacey, R.D. (2000) *Strategic management & organizational dynamics*, 3rd edition. The Challenge of Complexity. Harlow: Pearson Education Limited.

Stacey, R.D. (2012) Comment on debate article: Coaching psychology coming of age: The challenges we face in the messy world of complexity. *International Coaching Psychology Review*, Vol. 7, No. 1, pp. 91–95.

Stacey, R.D., Griffin, D. and Shaw, P. (2000) *Complexity and management. Fad or radical challenge to systems thinking*. London and New York: Routledge.

Stacey, R.D. and Mowles, C. (2016) *Strategic management and organisational dynamics: The challenge of complexity to ways of thinking about organisations*, 7th edition. Harlow, England: Pearson Education Limited.

Thurner, S., Hanel, R. and Klimek, P. (2018) *Introduction to the theory of complex systems* (p. 1). Oxford: Oxford University Press (Kindle edition).

Wells, J. (2013) *Complexity and sustainability. Routledge Studies in Ecological Economics*. New York: Routledge/Taylor and Francis (Kindle edition).

5 Project management and indigenous complexity-related concepts

Wicked problems

The wicked problems constituting a challenge for policy making, management, project management, and software development can be seen as representative for difficulties associated with all interpretations of complexity. The term "wicked problems" was described in detail for the first time in the paper on social policy (urban problems) published by Rittel and Weber (1973). The term had been coined earlier by Rittel and discussed in public by Churchman (1967). It must be added that the term "wicked" has no ethical connotation but rather is used as to add an emotionally laden perception of difficulty. Rittel and Weber (1973, p. 160) state that "wicked problems stand in opposition with "tame" or "benign" problems which occur in mathematics – solving a mathematical problem or identifying a structure in organic chemistry. The solution is found sooner or later or it is waiting for a genius. The wicked problems are not solvable at all in this manner.

The wicked problems were studied in detail in multiple works (e.g. Conklin 2006; Horn and Weber 2007; *Swedish Morphological Society* 2021); thus here only the meaning of complexity in the wicked problems is briefly explained. Although wicked problems were developed within the framework of systems analysis they can be treated as a fundamental methodological general issue.

In the abovementioned paper of Rittel and Weber the term complex is used only in an intuitive sense in relation to causal network, the workings of open societal systems, and the world of social policy making. More profound discussions on the links between the wicked problems and complexity were presented by Conklin (2006). His key concept is fragmentation which is defined as wickedness × social complexity. He does not treat wicked problems as complex by themselves but underscores the fact they occur in a complex social environment. He defines social complexity as a function of the number and diversity of players who are involved in a project (Conklin 2006, p. 12). The only reference to the complexity of projects in this work is presented when it is linked with non-linearity.

An opposite approach to wicked problems was proposed by Horn and Weber (2007). They admit that wicked problems are inherently so complex

DOI: 10.4324/9781003175032-6

that they cannot be understood anywhere near well enough to develop reasonable methods for making progress in resolving them. They propose their methodologies allowing the wicked problems to be solved. They use the idea proposed by Ackoff (1974, p. 21) who treats complex problems as messes:

> We have also come to realize that no problem ever exists in complete isolation. Every problem interacts with other problems and is therefore part of a set of interrelated problems, a system of problems I choose to call such a system a mess … Furthermore solutions to most problems produce other problems.

Horn and Weber (2007, p. 6) interpret social messes as wicked, ill-structured problems and the complexity of those messes is treated as equivalent to Systems of Systems.

A special systems methodology designated to deal with "wicked", "messy" problems called Strategic Assumption Surfacing and Testing (SAST) was developed by Mason and Mitroff (1981) for strategic management under the influence of the ideas of Churchman. In their interpretation, the wicked problems affect organized complexity, and they can be identified by the following facets: Interconnectedness to other problems, complexity with recursive feedback, uncertainty in a dynamic environment, ambiguity dependent on viewpoint, conflicting trade-offs of alternative solutions, and societal constraints to theoretical solutions. Every problem is inextricably united to the environment in which it is embedded.

Leaving the details of the SAST for more deepened considerations, two comments must be added. First, the SAST was developed with the full awareness of the fact that claims for a full understanding of any system are not realistic. Second, it must be always borne in mind that an idealistic interpretation of any systems methodology as providing a comprehensive, holistic understanding of a system is unachievable. Wicked problems perfectly reflect these limitations.

The wicked problems emerge in project management in dealing with all kinds of complex systems – organizations, projects, environment, etc.

When searching for the links between Agile Project Management and wicked problems it must be mentioned that the origins of Scrum are directly associated with wicked problems. They were introduced to software development by DeGrace and Stahl (1990) in their book where they also used the term scrum and which was another source of inspiration for the founders of Scrum as an Agile methodological framework (Schwaber and Beedle 2002, p. 11; Sutherland 2021, p. 16).

Synergetics of R. Buckminster Fuller

Contrary to a relatively well-defined set of ideas developed in physics by Hermann Haken and co-workers called synergetics, that was later transferred to other domains of knowledge, the synergetics created by R. Buckminster

Fuller constitutes a collection of a large variety of ideas. In the interpretation of Fuller, synergy means the behaviour of integral, aggregate, whole systems unpredicted by the behaviours of any of their components or subassemblies of their components taken separately from the whole. In a broader, universal sense, synergetics is interpreted as an inter- and multi-disciplinary idea demanding a relatively high level of understanding of a broad range of disciplines – philosophy, theology, mathematics (arithmetic and geometry), physics, architecture, chemistry, engineering, education, and environment. In a narrower sense, the dominant idea of Fuller was to link energy with geometry creating a specific spatial ordering: "Synergetics is energetic geometry since it identifies energy with number. Energetic geometry employs 60-degree coordination because that is nature's way to closest-pack spheres" (Fuller 1997).

The terms complex and complexity are frequently referred to in the ideas associated synergetics. In the most universal sense Fuller understands complexity as a property of spatial ordering analysed with various geometric constructs.

From the wealth of innovations created by Fuller, two conceptions can be recalled: A geometric structure called a tetrahedron defined by four closest-packed unit-radius spheres constitutes the central element of spatial structures, and tensegrity, a structural-relationship principle in which structural shape is guaranteed by the finitely closed, comprehensively continuous, tensional behaviours of the system (Fuller 1997). This latter concept has become very popular in architecture and construction.

This short description can be treated only as an introduction to the presentation of the examples of the relations between project management and Fuller's version of synergetics. Due to their scope and depth, his ideas require more profound studies of the following works (Fuller 1997; Edmondson 2007) and the website of the Buckminster Fuller Institute.

As was mentioned earlier, the synergetics of Buckminster Fuller was an important source of inspiration for the concepts of Team Syntegrity, in management cybernetics developed by Stafford Beer.

Hierarchies, holons, and fractals in project management

Hierarchical structure is one of the fundamental attributes of complexity of natural, social, and engineering systems. This role of the hierarchical nature of complex systems is not always studied with sufficient attention. Therefore it is worthwhile to recall briefly three areas where hierarchy is given special attention. The first area embodies classical hierarchies, but in the case of holons and fractal organization an additional explanation is necessary.

Hierarchies and complex systems

Internal hierarchies are an indispensable attribute of all kinds of systems, natural and artificial. Hierarchy in a general sense and especially in social systems may have a multitude of interpretations. Herbert Simon (1962, 1973) regarded internal hierarchy as the key to a better understanding of complex systems. Looking from a current perspective we may state that he tried to enrich an intuitive understanding of complexity with more advanced analyses referring to physics, biology, psychology, and cognitive science. In the study of relations between the internal hierarchy of systems and complexity, Lane (2006) distinguished the following types of hierarchy.

Order hierarchy is built with a characteristic describing a set of elements, e.g. numerical ordering, alphanumerical ordering, size. Order hierarchy does not even refer to relationships and interactions among the entities. In consequence this type of ordering does not influence the complexity of systems.

Inclusion hierarchy reflects the recursive character of belonging. Lane (2006) several times recalls Simon (1973, p. 5) who illustrated this type of hierarchy with the famous Chinese boxes.

> In application to the architecture of complex systems, "hierarchy" simply means a set of Chinese boxes of a particular kind. A set of Chinese boxes usually consists of a box enclosing a second box, which, in turn, encloses a third – the recursion continuing as long as the patience of the craftsman holds out. The Chinese boxes called "hierarchies" are a variant of that pattern. Opening any given box in a hierarchy discloses not just one new box within, but a whole small set of boxes; and opening any one of these component boxes discloses a new set in turn.

This means that entity is a container which includes other containers creating the inclusion hierarchy all the way down.

Control hierarchy is of special importance in social systems and fundamental in management. It is built by the possibilities of giving orders, or using a more relevant language, it is the structure of power sharing. Units at higher levels in this type of hierarchy have the possibility of influencing the behaviour of the units at the lower ranks.

Level hierarchy is created by observers as a collection of units existing at different levels characterized by a specific spatio-temporal scale. The higher the level, the more extended is the associated spatio-temporal scale. Entities at a given level, through their interactions, may construct the elements at the higher level in a process called upward causation. The level hierarchies through upward causation may create inclusion hierarchy. At the same time entities at the higher level hierarchy may exert impact on the entities at the lower level. This phenomenon is called downward causation. A biological example of level hierarchy: Cells – organs – individuals – species, and an example from management: Individuals – units – departments – company.

The above introductory descriptions leave open a multitude of questions. What are the patterns of interactions within the levels of hierarchy and between the levels? Are the elements interacting directly only with closest neighbours? What are the relations between the whole and the element? What information do the interacting elements possess? Is it only information about the closest neighbourhood? These questions can be multiplied.

Holons

When studying human social systems an important question arises. We already know about emerging properties and hierarchies in physics, chemistry, and biology. We also to some extent know how structured patterns of behaviour emerge in biological collectivities, e.g. birds and bees thanks to the studies of boids initiated by Reynolds (1987). However, in the models of life and of the collective behaviour of human social systems other factors have to be considered like, for example, the complexity of elements at each level of the hierarchy, e.g. organism vs. molecules, social groups vs. states, relations between elements at various levels of hierarchy, relations between the levels of hierarchy. When studying society we have to think about the impact of the awareness of conscious humans of the relations between them and society. Humans are not boids; when acting individually we know at least partly about the impact on our deeds on society and vice versa.

An attempt to answer at least some of these philosophical and practical questions was made by Arthur Koestler (1967). His idea of holons is rooted in the fundamental philosophical problem of explaining the sense of relations between whole, parts, and hierarchy in biological and social collectivities. Koestler also found inspiration for his concept in the parable of two watchmakers invented by Simon (1962) in which the watches (systems) produced by a watchmaker using a hierarchical approach and building watches with intermediate-level modules are less prone to disturbances than the products of a watchmaker who build watches (systems) without constructing collective elements at the intermediate level of hierarchy.

Koestler wanted to show two things with this parable. First, that complex systems will evolve from simple systems much more rapidly if there are stable intermediate forms than if there are not, i.e. if they are hierarchically organized. Second, and more importantly, he wants to show that the resulting complex systems will always be hierarchic and that hierarchy is the natural and ubiquitous outcome of the development of structural form (Edwards 2003).

In the simplest way the word holon is a combination of the Greek "*holos*" meaning whole, with the suffix "on" which, as in proton or neutron, suggests a particle or part. The holon, then, is a part-whole. It is a nodal point in a hierarchy that describes the relationship between entities that are self-complete wholes and entities that are seen to be other dependent parts. As one's point of focus moves up, down, and/or across the nodes of a hierarchical structure so one's perception of what is a whole and what is a part will also change (Edwards 2003).

The holons constitute a specific kind of hierarchy, i.e. holarchy. A holarchy or hierarchy is a system of holons at different levels. In this system lower level holons compose a higher level holon, and a higher level holon comprises lower level holons. Any holon is a part with regard to the higher level holon it composes, and at the same time a whole with regard to the lower level holon(s) it comprises. Therefore, a holon is a part/whole. The analogy with the Chinese boxes and with Russian dolls can be used as an illustration. For example, an organ is a part of an organism, but a whole with regard to the cells of which it is comprised. The hierarchical systems of holons were called by Koestler Open Hierarchical Systems (OHS). Their features are described in detail in Appendix 1 of his book *The Ghost in the Machine* (Koestler 1967, pp. 341–348). From a managerial point of view, the important characteristics of the OHS are depth and scope. The number of levels which a hierarchy comprises is a measure of its "depth", and the number of holons on any given level is called its "span" (Simon) (Koestler 1967, p. 342).

References to holons in project management are not too frequent yet. Two examples in which the idea of holons is applied in project management both derive from Agile manufacturing and Agile management. The concept of holonic manufacturing developed by Hendrik van Brussel in reducing uncertainty in project management was used by Bakos and Dumitrașcu (2017). They enriched the applications of complex adaptive systems in project risk management with Koestler's holarchy-related ideas. Dalton (2019) in his book on managing Agile enterprises treats applications of holons as the direction of future development of Agile management including project management and product development.

Fractals in project management

Selected examples relating to fractals and Agile are the following:

1. Agile project life cycle as fractal in which all stages of the process are treated as fractals (Sliger 2008).
2. Fractal Agile Metamodel (FRAME) (Sadi and Ramsin 2009) in which the adaptive process framework developed in the ASD (Highsmith 2000, 2010) and Crystal Clear (Cockburn 2005, 2007) methodologies is enhanced by defining a metamodel incorporating adaptability into the process framework. Moreover, FRAME models all the activities performed in an Agile process, from the top-most enterprise management activities, to Agile Project Management and the fine-grained Agile practices and activities, all with the same simple self-similar metamodel. In this way the idea of adaptive frameworks is generalized by introducing an all-encompassing fractal metamodel for Agile processes in management.

Complexity of social systems: The concepts of Niklas Luhmann

Although developed as a broad sociological theory, the concept of social system developed by Niklas Luhmann has gained significant influence in management theory, especially in Europe. The theory of social systems is built on the idea of autopoiesis proposed by Maturana and Varela (1980) in theoretical biology. According to Luhmann, a social system can be treated as a system of meaningful communication. A complex system is one in which there are more possibilities than can be actualized. Complexity of operations means that the number of possible relations becomes too large with respect to the capacity of elements to establish relations. It means that complexity enforces selection. The other concept of complexity is defined as a problem of observation. Now, if a system has to select its relations itself, it is difficult to foresee what relations it will select, for even if a particular selection is known, it is not possible to deduce which selections would be made (Luhmann, 1990, p. 81). As an example the survey of applications of Luhmann's ideas in organization theory can be recalled (Seidl and Becker 2006).

Self-observation and self-reflexivity were introduced in the studies of Heinz von Foerster, Humberto Maturana, and Francisco Varela devoted to self-organization in social systems. As is already known, self-organization constitutes one of the key issues in Agile Project Management. Von Foerster developed his own theory of self-organization deriving from thermodynamics and information theory. In his concept self-organization results from informational noise in the system (von Foerster 1982). A short reminder about this idea is necessary in further considerations on self-organization in Agile Project Management. For the same purposes the concept of *autopoiesis* of Maturana and Varela is recalled. A neologism, *autopoiesis* (from Greek αὐτο- (*auto-*), meaning "self", and ποίησις (*poiesis*), meaning "creation, production") refers to a system capable of reproducing and maintaining itself. *Autopoiesis* was designed for the study of biological systems – biological cells – and in the most synthetic way it can be defined as follows: An autopoietic machine is a machine organized (defined as a unity) as a network of processes of production (transformation and destruction) of components which: (i) Through their interactions and transformations continuously regenerate and realize the network of processes (relations) that produced them; and (ii) constitute it (the machine) as a concrete unity in space in which they (the components) exist by specifying the topological domain of its realization as such a network (Maturana and Varela 1980, p. 78).

Autopoiesis was transferred to sociology by Niklas Luhmann as a foundation of his theory of social systems (Luhmann 2013). At present it is also applied in multiple concepts of management. However, it is necessary to remember that Maturana and Varela (1980, p. xxiii) were critical about the use of their idea taken from biology to study social systems. It was also criticized by other authors (Scott 2021, p. 62). However, looking at the present tendencies and multitude of interpretations, it may be concluded that applications of *autopoiesis* in social sciences are living their own life. It is recalled here in an introductory way to demonstrate the relations between the ideas of Luhmann, von Foerster, Maturana, and Varela and Pask.

References to the works of Luhmann have become an important source of inspiration in project management and in Agile Project Management. As an example the projects of Saynisch and the idea of Project Management Second (PM2) can be recalled in which the ideas of Luhmann are referred to (Saynisch 2010, 2010a).

References

Ackoff, R.L. (1974) *Redesigning the future: A systems approach to societal problems*. New York: John Wiley & Sons.

Bakos, L. and Dumitraşcu, D.D. (2017) *Holonic handling the unexpected in project management*. https://ideas.repec.org/a/vrs/brcebe/v3y2017i1p137-143n19.html.

Churchman, C.W. (1967) Guest editorial: Wicked problems. *Management Science*, Vol. 14, No. 4, pp. B141–B142. doi: 10.1287/mnsc.14.4.B141.

Cockburn, A. (2005) *Crystal Clear. A human-powered methodology for small teams*. Boston, MA: Addison-Wesley.

Cockburn, A. (2007). *Agile Software Development: The cooperative game*. (Agile Software Development Series) . Boston: Pearson Education. Kindle Edition.

Conklin, J. (2006) *Dialogue mapping: Building shared understanding of wicked problems*. Chichester: John Wiley & Sons.

Dalton, J. (2019) *Great big agile: An OS for agile leaders*. Waterford, MI: Apress.

DeGrace, P. and Stahl, L.H. (1990) *Wicked problems, righteous solutions: A catalogue of modern software engineering paradigms*. Englewood Cliffs, NJ: Yourdon Press.

Edmondson, A.C. (2007) *A fuller explanation: The synergetic geometry of R. Buckminster Fuller* (Back-In-Action Edition). Pueblo, CO: Emergent World Press.

Edwards, M., (2003) A brief history of holons, *Integral World*, https://www.integralworld.net/edwards13.html

Fuller, R. B. (in collaboration with E.J. Applewhite) (1997) *Synergetics: Explorations in the geometry of thinking*. Online edition hosted by R.W. Gray, originally published by Macmillan, Vol. 1 in 1975 (with a preface and contribution by Arthur L. Loeb; ISBN 0-02-541870-X), Vol. 2 in 1979 (ISBN 0025418807). http://www.rwgrayprojects.com/synergetics/synergetics.html.

Highsmith, J.A. III (2000) *Adaptive software development. A collaborative approach to managing complex systems*. New York: Dorset House Publishing Co. (Kindle edition)

Highsmith, J.R. (2010) *Agile project management: Creating innovative products*, 2nd edition. Boston: Pearson Education.

Horn, R.E. and Weber, R.P. (2007) *New tools for resolving wicked problems. Mess mapping and resolution mapping processes*. MacroVU(r), Inc. and Strategy Kinetics, LLC. https://www.strategykinetics.com//New_Tools_For_Resolving_Wicked_Problems.pdf.

Koestler, A. (1967) *The ghost in the machine*. New York: The Macmillan Company.

Lane, D. (2006) Hierarchy, complexity, society. In D. Pumain (ed.), *Hierarchy in natural and social sciences*. Methodos Series, Vol 3. Dordrecht: Springer, pp. 81–119. doi: 10.1007/1-4020-4127-6_5.

Luhmann, N. (1990). *Essays on Self-Reference*. New York: Columbia University Press.

Luhmann, N. (2013) *Introduction to systems theory*. Cambridge: Polity.

Maturana, H. and Varela, F. (1980) *Autopoiesis and cognition. The realisation of the living*. Boston Studies in the Philosophy of Science # 42. Boston, MA: Riedel Publishing.

Mason, R.O. and Mitroff, I.I. (1981) *Challenging strategic planning assumptions: Theory, cases and techniques*. Chichester: Wiley-Interscience.

Reynolds, C.W. (1987) Flocks, herds, and schools: A distributed behavioral model. *Computer Graphics*, Vol. 21, No. 4, pp. 25–34. doi: 10.1145/37402.37406.

Rittel, H.W.J. and Webber, M.M. (1973) Dilemmas in a general theory of planning. *Policy Sciences*, Vol. 4, pp. 155–169. doi: 10.1007/BF01405730.

Sadi, M.H. and Ramsin, R. (2009) FRAME: A generic fractal process metamodel for agile methodologies. In R. Lee and N. Ishii (eds), *Software engineering research. Management and applications. Studies in computational intelligence*, Vol. 253. Berlin, Heidelberg: Springer, pp. 251–264. doi: 10.1007/978-3-642-05441-9_22.

Saynisch, M. (2010) Beyond frontiers of traditional project management: An approach to evolutionary, self-organizational principles and the complexity theory—results of the research program. *Project Management Journal*, Vol. 41, No. 2, pp. 21–37. https://doi.org/10.1002/pmj.20159

Saynisch, M. (2010a) Mastering complexity and changes in projects, economy, and society via project management second order (pm-2), *Project Management Journal*, Vol. 41,No. 5, pp. 4–20. https://doi.org/10.1002/pmj.20167

Schwaber, K. and Beedle, M. (foreword by Jeff Sutherland) (2002) *Agile software development with Scrum*. Upper Saddle River, NJ: Prentice Hall.

Scott, B. (2021) *Cybernetics for the social sciences*. Leiden and Boston, MA: Brill.

Seidl, D. and Becker, K.H. (2006) Organizations as distinction generating and processing systems: Niklas Luhmann's contribution to organization studies. *Organization*, Vol. 13, No. 1, pp. 9–35.

Simon, H.A. (1962) The architecture of complexity. *Proceedings of the American Philosophical Society*, Vol. 106, No. 6, pp. 467–482.

Simon, H.A. (1973) The organization of complex systems. In H. Pattee (ed.), *Hierarchy theory: The challenge of complex systems*. New York: George Braziller, pp. 3–27.

Sliger, M. (2008) *Agile project management and the PMBOK® guide*. Paper presented at PMI® Global Congress 2008—North America, Denver, CO. Newtown Square, PA: Project Management Institute. https://www.pmi.org/learning/library/agile-project-management-pmbok-waterfall-7042.

Sutherland J. (2021) *The Scrum papers: Nuts, bolts, and origins of an Agile framework*, Lincoln MA, https://www.scruminc.com/scrumpapers.pd.f

Swedish Morphological Society (2021) Decision support modelling with morphological analysis. http://www.swemorph.com/

Von Foerster, H. (1982) *Observing systems. A collection of papers by Heinz von Foerster*. Seaside, CA: Inter-Systems Publications.

6 Scrum and complexity-related ideas

Introduction

Undoubtedly complexity-related ideas exerted a decisive impact on the origins and development of Scrum. To understand this impact more profoundly, we have scrutinized the entire process of applications of those ideas in Scrum, beginning from the origins of Scrum and ending with the present-day status (mid-2021). Our main sources of information are the various types of publications – books, scientific papers, conference papers, websites, and blogs of the founders of Scrum and of their associates. Whenever needed, we quote other authors presenting information and their views about Scrum and its relations with complexity-related ideas.

A thorough analysis of the links between complexity-related ideas and the development of Scrum allows for the identification of two periods. The first one, studied in this chapter, began with the first appearances of the publications on Scrum from the mid-1990s until the end of the first decade of the 21st century. The borderline is not absolutely rigid and there may be some exceptions, e.g. Sutherland (2012) and other works. The second period, comprising a part of the second decade of the 21st century until mid-2021, is represented by the publications of the founders of Scrum and other authors and institutions who were applying Scrum with the input of complexity-related concepts. The choice of the periods is not incidental since from the beginnings of the second decade of the 21st century we can observe significant changes in the status of complexity-related ideas in Scrum.

The ideas of Scrum were presented to a broad audience for the first time in 1995 in a paper during the Object-Oriented Programming, Systems, Languages & Applications (OOPSLA) conference of the Association of Computing Machinery (Schwaber 1995). In an extended version the paper was later published (Schwaber 1997). The founders of Scrum published three books in the first decade of the 21st century (Schwaber and Beedle 2002; Schwaber 2004, 2009; Sutherland 2010). Additionally, the collections of Scrum Papers reflecting the status of knowledge about Scrum in the subsequent years began to appear in 2007, 2011, 2012, and in 2021. In our study we refer solely to the

DOI: 10.4324/9781003175032-7

most recent collection of the Scrum Papers (Sutherland 2021) because the earlier versions of the Scrum Papers are no longer available on the Internet.

To assess preliminarily the role of complexity-related ideas in the origins of Scrum, the results of a survey of initial fundamental works on Scrum (Schwaber 1995) (published in 1997); Schwaber 1996; Schwaber and Beedle 2002; Sutherland 2021; Schwaber 2004, 2009) are described and interpreted. In the case of the book of Schwaber, both versions were scrutinized and it is reflected in the respective quotations. The aim of the survey was to identify the occurrences and interpretations of the notions (alphabetic order): Adaptation, adaptive, chaos, complex, complexity, complex adaptive systems, complexities, edge of chaos, emergence, and self-organization in the body of the above texts. The impact of complexity studies on Scrum was also mirrored in other works but due to their importance, the works of the founders of Scrum were treated as the primary area of our research.

The number and size of the texts under scrutiny did not demand more advanced methods of processing applied in research on the language corpora and in interpretations of metaphors. The survey is only partly elaborated with computer support (identification of occurrences). The interpretations of the abovementioned terms are primarily analysed. Such an approach is additionally justified due to the variety of complexity-related terms. It lays the grounds for further more rigorous linguistic and theoretical considerations.

A question arises: What were the sources of inspiration and knowledge about complexity-related ideas in the aforementioned initial works on Scrum? The development and popularization of broadly defined complexity studies (1980s and 1990s) coincided with the publication of the first ideas of Scrum (Schwaber 1995, 1996, 1997). The following works connected with broadly defined complexity-related ideas were treated as the sources of inspiration and new knowledge in the pioneer publications on Scrum:

- Schwaber (1995/1997): Takeuchi and Nonaka (1986), Gleick (1987), Langton (1989) (quoted therein as published in 1988) Correct year 1989 – it is quoted like that in the book.
- Schwaber (1996): Gleick (1987), Raccoon (1995)
- Schwaber and Beedle (2002): Holland (1995, 1998), Kauffman (1993), Senge (1990), Stacey (1996), Takeuchi and Nonaka (1986), Ogunnaike and Ray (1994)
- Schwaber (2004, 2009): Stacey (1993), Stacey *et al.* (2000) – this position was quoted as a part of the Routledge Series "Complexity and Emergence in Organizations"
- Sutherland (2021): Senge (1990), Langton (1992), Holland (1995, 1998)

The founders of Scrum treated the paper of Takeuchi and Nonaka (1986) as one of their main sources of inspiration. In the paper, the term scrum, deriving from scrum (scrummage) – a method of restarting play in rugby football reflecting a metaphor of self-organization – was proposed, and the ideas of complex systems of Prigogine (1980), Jantsch (1981), and self-organization (Sahal 1979) were used as the source of ideas in devising a new approach to product development. Sutherland (2010, p. 62) called Takeuchi and Nonaka the godfathers of Scrum to expose their role in its origins. The term scrum in project management has also other roots. It was used by DeGrace and Stahl (1990) in their book titled *Wicked Problems, Righteous Solutions*, who found inspiration in the paper of Takeuchi and Nonaka (1986). It was mentioned several times by the founders of Scrum (Schwaber and Beedle 2002, p. 11; Sutherland 2021, p. 16).

An important source of ideas associated with systems thinking and indirectly with understanding of complexity was the concept of Observe-Orient-Decide-Act (OODA) of John Boyd, a fighter pilot and specialist in military strategy and business strategy (Richards 2004). According to Sutherland (2012) OODA constituted another source of inspiration for the creators of Scrum.

Scrum and complexity

Applications of complexity-related ideas in Scrum must be viewed in a broader context of the influence of the studies of complexity and of complex adaptive systems (CAS) in particular. It was already exposed in the first publication on Scrum that the main feature of this methodological framework proposed for software development was the ability of adaptation which derives from the universal principles of evolution. It was underscored that software development teams in Scrum had a significant ability to adapt to rapidly changing complex environments (Schwaber 1995/1997).

When conducting our research we are trying to answer the most fundamental question: Did the founders of Scrum claim directly that any of systems under study, i.e. software projects, project teams, organizations which develop the project, and customer organizations, are complex adaptive systems according to their definitions or are they treated solely as metaphors and analogies? The answer is not unequivocal. From the discussions on complex adaptive systems a specific duality is emerging. It can be claimed that a collectivity (project, project team, organization) is a complex adaptive system if it is possible to develop its mathematical model, as for example those developed by Holland (1995). In the case when the term complex adaptive system is used only in qualitative terms, without any operationalized components, it can be considered that it is used only in the sense of metaphor and analogy. We leave for a further discussion the idea of complexity of organization presented in the concept of CRPR developed by Stacey and his co-workers (Stacey 2000; Stacey *et al.* 2000) and discussed in Chapter 4.

Following the assumptions of our study, in this part we present the uses of the notions complex and complexity in the fundamental works on Scrum (Schwaber 1995 (published version of 1997); Schwaber 1996, Schwaber and Beedle 2002; Schwaber 2004 also edition 2009; Sutherland 2021).

In the first work, where the main ideas of Scrum were presented publicly in a comprehensive way (Schwaber 1995/1997), the notions complex and complexity are mentioned multiple times. In the paper directly referring to edge of chaos (Schwaber 1996) the terms complex and complexity appear several times in different contexts. In the book of Schwaber and Beedle (2002) complex and complexity are treated as attributes of projects, people, and environment. In this book a new approach to complexity is presented linking it with noise. In the fundamental book on Scrum (Schwaber 2004, 2009), the terms complex and complexity are applied about 50 times. A simplified version of the Stacey Matrix is included both in Schwaber and Beedle (2002, p. 93) and in Schwaber (2004, p. 5; 2009, p. 27). It is interesting to observe that the plural term complexities can be found multiple times in Schwaber (2004, 2009).

The ideas concerning Scrum were summarized in the publication: "The Scrum Papers: Nuts, Bolts, and Origins of an Agile Process". Due to the reasons mentioned earlier, we scrutinized only the 2021 edition of the Scrum Papers (Sutherland 2021). Selected examples of applications of interpretations of the terms complex and complexity in the first works on Scrum are presented in Table 6.1.

As was mentioned earlier, it is assumed that all applications of complexity-related ideas in all Agile methodological frameworks are treated as analogies and metaphors. Additionally, at this stage of research, we do not apply any systematic methodologies of identification of metaphors as, for example (Steen *et al.* 2010). When studying the applications of the terms complex and complexity in the early publications on Scrum, the following questions will be asked:

1) What types of interpretations of the terms complex and complexity were applied?
2) What were their source fields and target fields when they are treated as metaphors?
3) What were the types and functions of terms complex and complexity used as metaphors?

The information included in Table 6.1 shows that the founders of Scrum use the terms complex and complexity in a wide range of interpretations. Two basic types of interpretations can be distinguished: First, intuitive interpretations according to which almost all characteristics of Scrum (project, team, people, environment) are affected by not too precisely defined complexity; and second, metaphors connected by the authors with broadly defined complexity theory.

Looking at the list of references in the five positions under scrutiny – see the list in the introduction to this chapter – we can see that numerous important positions from complexity-related literature are quoted. Studying the uses of the terms complex and complexity directly referring to complexity science, for example, a sentence from Table 6.1: Complexity management, that is, in self-organization, management of empirical processes, and knowledge creation…

Table 6.1 Selected complexity-related utterances in the first publications on Scrum

Complex	**Complex** – environment, products, projects, system (in a general sense), system development process, unpredictable environments, work (*multiple occurrences*).
	Complicated and **complex** system development process, 1, p. 8.
	Developing **complex** software feels like running an obstacle course. Agility, flexibility, and adaptability are required to succeed, 3, p. 99.
	Software development is a **complex** endeavour, 4, p. 22.
	The **complex** process by which pressure turns coal into diamonds, 4, p. 22.
	The interaction of the most **complex** organisms on the planet – people, 4, p. 22.
	Complex problems are those that behave unpredictably, 4, p. 23.
Complexity	We relate Scrum to **complexity** theory, 1, p. 1
	The overall **complexity** is a function: *Complexity = f(development environment variables + target environment variables)*, 1, p. 4.
	Complexity of the variables as the factor diminishing the probability of a "successful" project (using any of the Waterfall, Spiral, or Iterative processes), 1, p. 7.
	Complexity, chaos, flexibility, and adaptability are connected, 1, p. 8.
	Complexity theory of Langton (1989) ("artificial life") as the source of inspiration, 1, p. 8.
	The project remains open to environmental **complexity**, including competitive, time, quality, and financial pressures, 1, p. 10; 2, p. 8.
	The empirical approach has been used by these independent software vendors (ISVs) to cope with the overwhelming degree of **complexity** and uncertainty – chaos – in which they develop products, 2, p. 3.
	We find the **complexity** and urgency of requirements coupled with the rawness and instability of technology to be daunting, 3, p. 2.
	Scrum asks people to try to wrest a predictable product from unpredictable **complexity**, 3, p. 51.
	Complexity theory can be seen as a whole new understanding of the causes and patterns of noise, 3, p. 90.
	The **complexity** of individuals and individuals working in teams raises the noise level for all projects, 3, pp. 93–94.
	This process (successfully developing software), Scrum, is devised specifically to wrest usable products from **complex** problems, 4, p. 22.
	Complexity of the intermediate activities, 4, p. 24.
	Requirements **complexity** and technology **complexity**, 4, p. 26.
	The third dimension of **complexity** is the people developing the software ... These people then start to work together, and the **complexity** level goes through the roof, 4, p. 27.
	Scrum addresses the **complexity** of software development projects by implementing the inspection, adaptation, and visibility requirements of empirical process control, 4, p. 27
	Complexity theory as the source of inspiration, 4, p. 211.
	The concepts of **complexity theory** are introduced along with the important distinction between empirical and predictive processes, 5, p. 54.
	Complexity drivers: Increasing problem **complexity**, increasing solution **complexity**, increasing technical **complexity** increasing compliance **complexity**, increasing team **complexity**, 5, pp. 100–101.
	Complexity management, that is, in self-organization, the management of empirical processes, and knowledge creation ... Scrum is not only a "parallel iterative and incremental" development method, it is also an "adaptive" software development method, 5, p. 222.

(*Continued*)

Table 6.1 Continued

Example of parallel occurrence (complex and complexity)	When **complex** things interact, the level of **complexity** goes through the roof … **Complexity** in software development has three significant dimensions: Requirements, technology, and people … The requirements of customers are **complex** because they are not only ambiguous, but also constantly changing … To compound the **complexity** of technology, more than one piece is usually employed, and the interfaces of the many are far more **complex** than the **complexity** within any single piece, 4, p. 26.
Complexities	Because of the nature of software development, there is no shortage of **complexities**, and there is no way to resolve them without hard work, intelligence, and courage, 4, p. 23; the project not only had **complexities**, but resolving each **complexity** required different levels of skill, intensity, and persistence, 4, p. 85.

Source: Own research based on: ([1] Schwaber 1995; [2] Schwaber 1996; [3] Schwaber and Beedle 2002; [4] Schwaber 2009; [5] Sutherland 2021).

Scrum is not only a "parallel iterative and incremental" development method, it is also an "adaptive" software development method". If complex and complexity are treated as metaphors then how can the reader of those works identify the relations between the source domain – very broadly defined complexity theory and the target domains? The fundamental text of Takeuchi and Nonaka (1986) can be connected with complexity theory, while Ogunnaike and Ray (1994) is more specific.

This example shows that the notions complex and complexity were used in the initial texts of the founders of Scrum as fuzzily defined metaphors. Obviously, we have only the texts and it was expected that the readers studied the sources by themselves and in result were/are able to build their pictures of relations between source domains and target domains.

There may also be another option: It could be assumed that some of the uses of the terms complex and complexity were not purely intuitive interpretations of complexity metaphors but were treated by the authors as at least partly deriving from complexity theory in the sense presented in the works referring to that theory.

The intuitive interpretations demand much more advanced linguistic considerations and they are not important for our research purposes. Before scrutinizing the functions of the terms complex and complexity treated as metaphors deriving from vaguely presented complexity theory, it must be admitted that it is not possible to guess the knowledge of the readers concerning the quoted works. If they are familiar with at least some of them then the functions of those metaphors are different than in the case where the readers are not too familiar with those ideas. It must be added that some of the quoted works (e.g. Langton 1989, 1992; Kaufmann 1993, 1995) include relatively advanced mathematical models. In such case, other works on complexity, such as Raccoon (1995), Stacey (1996), and predominantly Gleick (1987), use complex and complexity as metaphors defined in a more precise way. It is impossible to guess to what extent the readers would develop their understanding of complex and complexity using only those works without delving into, for example, subtleties between interpretations of complexity proposed by Kauffman (1993, 1995) – mathematical models – and Stacey (1996).

The above analysis leads to the conclusion that, due to limited possibilities of identification of the source domains and their relations with the target domains, the functions of the terms complex and complexity treated as conceptual metaphors were only partly exploited in the first works on Scrum. When the terms complexity and complex are viewed as deliberate metaphors as defined by Steen (2008) the conclusion is similar.

A different conclusion can be drawn when complex and complexity described in the first works on Scrum are treated as persuasive terms. In this case it can be easily observed that the world presented in those works is overwhelmingly complex. It derives both from intuitive interpretations of complexity and metaphors and analogies referring to complexity theory as well as from the complexity-related models used in some of the quoted publications, for example (Langton 1989, 1992; Kauffman 1993, 1995).

Such an overwhelming vision of the complex reality of software development brings about some performative consequences. The authors describe and create a vision of complex projects, teams, environment, and people. Due to imprecision in reference to the source domains and target domains of complex and complexity metaphors and the number and character of intuitive interpretations, the authors create a new complex world of Scrum and of its environment.

The performative character of complex and complexity of all aspects of Scrum leads to another question. What are the intentions of the authors of Scrum and what are the main stimuli of persuasion associated with the terms complex and complexity? Following (Sopory and Dillard 2002), a preliminary answer can be deduced from the number and wealth of references to complexity – intuitive interpretations, e.g. complexity going through the roof and complexity-theory based interpretations. It is the creators of Scrum who in reaction to overwhelming complexity found in universally understood software development propose a new comprehensive approach allowing them to cope with that phenomenon. Such an approach is absolutely normal for innovators introducing new ideas. It is of special importance in training and in the practice of management/project management.

Scrum, chaos, and the edge of chaos

Chaos and the edge of chaos were also frequently used in the first works on Scrum. Although the names are similar the origins are different. As was mentioned in Chapter 4, the term chaos was used purposively for a class of mathematical models (Li and Yorke 1975). The term edge of chaos, associated with the modelling of artificial life with cellular automata, was coined by Langton (1989, 1992) and popularized by Waldrop (1992, pp. 230–231). The works of Langton were quoted by Schwaber (1995/1997) and Sutherland (2021).

Additionally, quotations of Gleick (1987) by Schwaber (1995/1997, 1996) prove their familiarity with the ideas of chaos theory. The examples of applications of those notions in the early works on Scrum are presented in Table 6.2.

Using the same methodological approach as for applications of complex and complexity in the first works on Scrum we may conclude that chaos and the edge of chaos are also used as intuitive terms. However, contrary to complex and complexity, chaos and the edge of chaos are applied predominantly as metaphors referring to complexity science. The transfer from the source field to the target field is not clear and is somehow indirect. The founders of Scrum were familiar with some of the classical works on complexity and chaos, but the description of relations between the source fields and target fields is unclear.

In consequence, as in the case of complex and complexity, chaos and the edge of chaos are conceptual and deliberate metaphors. It may not be concluded that they are performative utterances – how to create chaos? Undoubtedly, they can be treated as an instrument of persuasion, as in the case of complex and complexity. There exists a very specific feature of chaos and the edge of chaos when treated as metaphors. Due to the initial meaning of those terms both of them have a strong emotional appeal. This was reflected in a paper by Langosco (2012): "Dealing with the Edge of Chaos Using Emotional, Cultural and Spiritual Intelligence".

Scrum, adaptation, emergence, self-organization

As was already mentioned, applications of the notion Scrum as a pattern and metaphor of self-organization have two sources of inspiration. The most important one is the paper of Takeuchi and Nonaka (1986), and the second, already mentioned, the book of DeGrace and Stahl (1991). We focus on self-organization as the pattern of behaviour of the product development team exposed by Takeuchi and Nonaka (1986). They built their concept on the metaphor drawn from rugby's scrum (scrummage). In their interpretation, the self-organizing project team has three properties: Autonomy, self-transcendence, and cross-fertilization. Self-organization derives from the following assumption:

> A project team takes on a self-organizing character as it is driven to a state of "zero information"—where prior knowledge does not apply. Ambiguity and fluctuation abound in this state. Left to stew, the process begins to create its own dynamic order.

Takeuchi and Nonaka (1986, p. 139) build this assumption on a broad metaphorical interpretation of the ideas of self-organization drawn from the works of classics of complexity studies – Nicolis and Prigogine (1977), Jantsch

Table 6.2 Selected chaos and edge of chaos-related utterances in the first publications on Scrum

Producing orderly systems under **chaotic** circumstances requires maximum flexibility. The closer the development team operates to the **edge of chaos**, while still maintaining order, the more competitive and useful the resulting system will be. Langton (1989) has modelled this effect in computer simulations, and his work has provided this as a fundamental theorem **in complexity theory**, 1, p. 8
Complexity, **edge of chaos**, and probability of success, 1, p. 9; accordingly, controls, including risk management, are put on each iteration of the Sprint phase to avoid **chaos** while maximizing flexibility, 1, p. 10
Operating at the **edge of chaos** (unpredictability and **complexity**) requires management controls to avoid falling into **chaos**, 1, p. 14
Controlled **chaos**: Living on the Edge, 2, p. 1; the **chaos** exists not only in the marketplace but in the technology. ISVs succeed and thrive amidst **chaos**, 2, p. 3
Several of the characteristics that guide Microsoft's **controlled-chaos** approach to the development process are inherent in Scrum, 2, p. 3; a Scrum software project is controlled by establishing, maintaining, and monitoring key control parameters. These controls are critical when software development encompasses an unknown quantity of uncertainty, unpredictable behaviour, and **chaos**, 2, p. 6
The very best product possible will be built. Development will occur in a controlled environment, as close to the **edge of chaos** as possible, 2, p. 7
Product increments are mined from **chaos,** 3, p. 51
Scrum has a self-organizing structure close to the **edge of chaos,** 3, p. 117
There is an optimum of adaptability in systems that self-organize close to the **edge of chaos**, 3, p. 118
The **chaos** in a company is often caused by an inability to resolve conflicting needs of sales and marketing departments, 4, p. 47
In software development organizations, **chaos** often results when a project's **complexity** is greater than its managers' ability to direct meaningful progress toward a goal. Scrum cuts through this kind of **complexity** and wrests order from **chaos**, 4, p. 72
"[Scrum] … allows teams to operate close to the '**edge of chaos**' to foster rapid system evolution, enforcing a simple set of rules for self-organization of software teams to produce systems with evolving architectures, aligning individual and organization objectives, creating a culture driven by performance, supporting shareholder value creation, achieving stable and consistent communication of performance at all levels, and enhancing individual development and quality of life", 5, p. 53
Concepts from artificial life (Langton 1992) are informative as systems that are flexible evolve faster as flexibility increases up to the boundary of **chaos**, 5, p. 54
The team must be able to execute the Sprint without being disrupted by project leaders, management, or other **chaos**-inducing forces in an organization, 5, p. 80
Scrum is an Agile software development process designed to add energy, focus, clarity, and transparency to project teams developing software systems. It leverages artificial life research (Langton 1992) by allowing teams to operate close to the **edge of chaos** to foster rapid system evolution, 5, p. 93

Source: Own research based on: ([1] Schwaber 1995/1997; [2] Schwaber 1996; [3] Schwaber and Beedle 2002; [4] Schwaber 2009; [5] Sutherland 2021).

(1981), and self-organization in cybernetics (Nonaka and Takeuchi 1986, p. 139). The second source of rugby-related inspiration for Scrum was the book by DeGrace and Stahl (1990) who, also referring to Takeuchi and Nonaka (1986), used the term Scrum in reference to software project development. In addition, indirectly, the approach to managing Agile Project Management was also influenced by systems thinking.

After the first analysis of the concepts of self-organization/self-organize/ self-organizing relating to teams in Scrum (Schwaber and Beedle 2002), they were scrutinized in the book by Schwaber (2004, 2009) and in the Scrum Papers by Sutherland (2021). Self-organization, emergence, and the empirical character of Scrum are treated as its essential novelty. In Schwaber (2004) self-organization occurs 23 times, self-organize 4 times, and self-organizing 7 times. According to Schwaber (2004, p. 1), the fundamental reason for exposing the role of self-organization of teams in Scrum is to increase the probability of the successful development of software by relevant complexity management – "to wrest usable products from complex problems". The self-organization of teams is also treated as the most relevant empirical project development approach as opposite to the front-end-loaded predictive approach.

The following questions concerning the self-organization of teams must be then asked: (1) What are the origins of the idea of self-organization? (2) What are the patterns of self-organization? (3) What is a metaphorical character of self-organization? (4) What are the sources of the normative character of self-organization?

The inspiration for using the term "self-organization" and related notions comes from four sources: First, indirect inspiration from complexity theory reflected in the references to Takeuchi and Nonaka (1986); second, direct reference to complex adaptive systems (Holland 1995, 1998) in the Scrum Papers (Sutherland 2021, p. 197); third, reference to industrial process control theory, which employs mechanisms such as self-organization and emergence in which no pre-defined process approach is applied (Ogunnaike and Ray 1994); and fourth, reference to the intuitive, hybrid interpretation of self-organization as a commonly known phenomenon.

When analysing the self-organization of Scrum teams, it is worthwhile to remember some facts. The Scrum Team includes the Product Owner, Development Team, and Scrum Master. According to all editions of Scrum Guide the optimum size of the Scrum Development Team is between three and nine members. Self-organization is a foundation of the work of the Scrum Development Team.

It is worthwhile to compare the patterns of self-organization from the source of complexity-inspired ideas of Scrum with the approach to self-organization in Scrum. Takeuchi and Nonaka (1986, p. 139) propose a project development approach in which self-organization begins from "zero information" and the team may define its own goal (goals). In the fundamental book on Scrum the self-organization of teams has the following features (Schwaber 2004): (1) Source of surprisingly high effectiveness, p. 21; (2) dividing the problems into manageable chunks, p. 23; (3) simplifying complexity and dealing with chaos – "Wrests order out of chaos", p. 37; (4) fostering creativity and worker satisfaction, p. 37; (5) coordinating dependencies of individuals, p. 45; (6) freeing commitments for common purpose, pp. 46, 48; (7) accompanying the empirical development of projects, p. 86; (8) self-organization as an emerging property, p. 86; (9) the Scrum Team assuming responsibility for planning its own work, p. 120; (10) facilitating self-management of the team, p. 102. Self-organizing teams are also the key factor of hyperproductivity achieved in Scrum (Sutherland 2021, p. 95, p. 96, p. 111).

In theoretical discussions on self-organization the key issue is the impact of external/internal dominant elements. In an abstract approach the initiation of self-organization should be spontaneous. However, in practice different patterns of influence may occur. In Scrum the role of Scrum Master is depicted with a relative high degree of precision. In all editions of Scrum Guides it is stated that: "not even the Scrum Master tells the Development Team how to turn Product Backlog into Increments of potentially releasable functionality". Additionally,

> The ScrumMaster (name used in the quoted books of Schwaber (2004, 2009), later used in a classical form) is responsible for the Scrum process, for teaching Scrum to everyone involved in the project, for implementing Scrum so that it fits within an organization's culture and still delivers the expected benefits, and for ensuring that everyone follows Scrum rules and practices.
>
> (Schwaber 2004, p. 7)

and spontaneous self-organization may be supported by simple rules devised by the ScrumMaster (Schwaber 2004, p. 132).

Self-organization is one of the instruments of making Scrum not predictive but an empirical approach in project development. According to Sutherland (2021, p. 234), from the Complexity Theory perspective (Holland 1995, 1998), Scrum allows flocking by forcing a faster agent interaction, therefore accelerating the process of self-organization because it shifts resources opportunistically through the daily Scrum Meetings.

References to self-organization as the key property of the Scrum Development Team deriving from complexity science are used in Scrum as dead metaphors. No direct correspondence between the characteristics of, say, complex adaptive systems and Scrum Development Teams can be found. Structural and functional characteristics of self-organization are not exposed. The statements that self-organization helps in complexity management are self-referential – self-organization is also an attribute of complexity. The exposition of learning as an instrument of self-organization does not only derive from complex systems. A more profound analysis of relations between the self-organizing Development Team, Scrum Master, and Product Owner shows that their relations are depicted without using any non-intuitive unequivocal correspondence (morphism) with the phenomena depicted in complexity science.

The normative and persuasive character of the dead metaphor of self-organization applied to Development Teams derives from its additional "scientific" value taken from complexity theory – nature is self-organizing and it is axiomatic that it must be effective in social phenomena. Both those normative approaches echo also Ashby's Law of Requisite Variety (Ashby 1957).

Self-organization is connected yet not identical with emergence, which is also one of the basic ideas of complexity science. A deep analysis of emergence as one of the characteristics of Scrum appeared for the first time in Schwaber (2004) and in Sutherland and Schwaber (2011). Reference to the role of emergence in industrial process control theory is made in a reference to (Ogunnaike and Ray 1994). In most cases emergence is mentioned together with self-organization.

According to Schwaber (2004), the following attributes of Scrum emerge in the process of software development: The tasks in the Sprint Backlog emerge as the Sprint evolves (p. 8), requirements for the product as the Product Backlog items (p.12), the productivity that emerges when a team figures out the best way to accomplish its goals (p. 28), and productive order as a result of team self-organization (p. 37).

In Sutherland (2021) the following examples of emergence are quoted: A list of tasks that defines a team's work for a Sprint. The list emerges during the Sprint (p. 32); software system with emergent, adaptive properties resembling the process of punctuated equilibrium observed in biological species (pp. 49); after one or more SyncSteps have been completed and forced some refactoring throughout the system, a new package of functionality emerges that is observable to the user, similar to genetic mutations (p. 88); "Emerging potion" resulting from mixing the flexibility and adaptability of Scrum with methods relevant to the disciplined and mature organization of project development, p. 128; highly emergent projects (little planning beyond the current Sprint), p. 163. The emergence of Backlog is also emphasized in all Scrum Guides.

The above considerations prove that in the initial works there were not any clearly defined direct correspondences between source domain (complexity theory) and target domain in applications of metaphors of self-organization and emergence. It can be only stated that the use of such vaguely defined terms could have some heuristic value – extension of the imagination stimulating language. Non-intuitive functional and structural correspondence between Scrum development and CAS cannot be identified. This phenomenon was already discussed in reference to the terms chaos and the edge of chaos. Enrichment of the normative vocabulary of Scrum with the term self-organization is helpful in improving processes depicted by a classical language of description of the various patterns of dynamics of any social collectivities.

Table 6.3 Selected self-organization and emergence-related utterances in the first publications on Scrum

Self-organization	[Scrum] Teams self-organize to turn the requirements and technology into product functionality, 1, p. 38 A project team takes on a self-organizing character as it is driven to a state of zero information, where prior knowledge does not apply, 1, p. 107. There is an optimum of adaptability in systems that self-organize right at the edge of chaos, 1, p. 118. Teams are self-managing, **self-organizing**, and cross-functional, and they are responsible for figuring out how to turn Product Backlog into an increment of functionality within an iteration and managing their own work to do so, 2, p. 30 I don't know why Scrum's **self-organization** works so well, but that hardly matters, 2, p. 52 …we'll see the power of time-boxing to instil the art of the possible and avoid the pursuit of perfection, the practice of incremental delivery to improve engineering practices, and the practice of empowerment and **self-organization** to foster creativity and worker satisfaction. 2, p. 72 **Self-organization** and human commitment are far more powerful mechanisms than imposed controls, plans, and even loyalty, 2, p. 83 For Scrum to work, the team has to deeply and viscerally understand collective commitment and **self-organization**, 2, p. 87 When the team members stop acting as many and adopt and commit to a common purpose, the team becomes capable of **self-organization** and can quickly cut through complexity and produce actionable plans, 2, p. 87 **Self-organizing** teams aren't unmanaged teams, 2, p. 151 We'll look at teams struggling to learn **self-organization** and self-management, 2, p. 157 Sometimes the Scrum Master can aid **self-organization** by devising a few simple rules, but it is easier for the Scrum Master to overdo it than not do enough, 2, p. 198 They (Takeuchi and Nonaka) described the best teams they had seen around the world as **self-organizing** teams characterized by autonomy, transcendence, and cross-fertilization, 3, p. 11 The Team in Scrum is "cross-functional" and is "self-organizing" (self-managing), 3, p. 18 It allows teams to operate close to the "edge of chaos" to foster rapid system evolution, enforcing a simple set of rules for **self-organization** of software teams to produce systems with evolving architectures, 3, p. 53 Scrum was designed to allow average developers to **self-organize** into high performance teams, 3, p. 95

(*Continued*)

Table 6.3 Continued

Emergence/emergent	Rules that are almost absurdly simple can generate coherent, emergent phenomena, 1, p. 115 The **emergent** nature of the Product Backlog, with focus on only the top-priority items, maximizes the probability that investment in detailing requirements is of value, 2, p. 219 A fully integrated component design environment leads to unexpected, rapid evolution of a software system with **emergent**, adaptive properties resembling the process of punctuated equilibrium observed in biological species, 3, p. 49 Thus **emergent** architecture, a core principle in all Agile processes, is not random evolution, 3, p. 89 This is understandable, because the relaxation of the **self-organized** multi-agent system is proportional to the average exchange among agents per unit of time. And in fact, the "interaction rate" is one of the levers one can push to control "emergent" behaviour – it is like adding an enzyme or catalyst to a chemical reaction, 3, p. 235
Emergence/ emergent and self-organization	This process, Scrum, is devised specifically to wrest usable products from **complex problems**. It has been used successfully on thousands of projects in hundreds of organizations over the last ten years. It is based on industrial process control theory, which employs mechanisms such as **self-organization** and **emergence**, 2, p. 22 People tend to interpret Scrum within the context of their current project management methodologies. They apply Scrum rules and practices without fully understanding the underlying principles of **self-organization**, **emergence**, and visibility and the inspection/adaptation cycle. They don't understand that Scrum involves a paradigm shift from control to empowerment, from contracts to collaboration, and from documentation to code, 2, p. 57 The dynamics of **self-organization**, collaboration, and **emergence** are best understood when a team faces a real problem, 2, p. 90 The words "empirical," "**self-organizing**," and "**emergent**" were virtually unknown in the program management office and would probably seem abhorrent to it, 2, p. 136

Source: Own research based on ([1] Schwaber and Beedle 2002; [2] Schwaber 2009; [3] Sutherland 2021).

References

Ashby, W.R. (1957) *An introduction to cybernetics*. London: Chapman & Hall.

DeGrace, P. and Stahl, L.H. (1990) *Wicked problems, righteous solutions: A catalogue of modern software engineering paradigms*. Englewood Cliffs, NJ: Yourdon Press.

Gleick, J. (1987) *Chaos: The making of a new science*. New York: Viking Press.

Holland, J.D. (1995) *Hidden order. How adaptation builds complexity*. New York: Basic Books.

Holland, J.D. (1998) *Emergence: From chaos to order*. Reading, MA: Addison-Wesley.

Jantsch, E. (1981) *The evolutionary vision: Toward a unifying paradigm of physical, biological, and sociocultural evolution*. Boulder, CO: Westview Press.

Kauffman, S.A. (1993) *The origins of order: Self-organization and selection in evolution*. New York and Oxford: Oxford University Press.

Kauffman, S.A. (1995) *At home in the universe. The search for laws of self-organization and complexity*. New York and Oxford: Oxford University Press.

Langosco, M. (2012) *Dealing with the edge of chaos using emotional, cultural and spiritual intelligence*. Paper presented at PMI® Global Congress 2012—EMEA, Marsailles, France. Newtown Square, PA: Project Management Institute, https://www.pmi.org/learning/library/dealing-edge-chaos-6433.

Langton, C. G. (1989) Artificial Life, in: C. G. Langton (ed), *Artificial Life: The Proceedings of an Interdisciplinary Workshop on the Synthesis and Simulation of Living Systems. SFI Studies in the Sciences of Complexity, Proceedings, Vol. 6*. Redwood City, CA: Addison-Wesley, pp. 1–48.

Langton, C.G. (1992). Life at the edge of chaos in: C. G. Langton, C. Taylor, J.D. Farmer and S. Rasmussen (eds), *Artificial Life II. Santa Fe Institute Studies in the Sciences of Complexity, Proceedings, vol. 10* (Proceedings of second Artificial Life workshop, 1990). Redwood City, CA: Addison-Wesley, pp. 41–91.

Li, T. -Y. and Yorke, J.A. (1975) Period three implies chaos. *The American Mathematical Monthly*, Vol. 82, No. 10, pp. 985–992.

Nicolis, G. and Prigogine, I. (1977) *Self-organization in nonequilibrium systems*. New York: Wiley Interscience.

Ogunnaike, B. , A. and Ray, W.H. (1994) *Process dynamics, modeling, and control*. Oxford, UK: Oxford University Press.

Prigogine, I. (1980) *From being to becoming. Time and complexity in the physical sciences*. New York: W. H. Freeman.

Raccoon, L.B.S. (1995) The chaos model and the chaos life cycle, ACM SIGSOFT. *Software Engineering Notes*, Vol. 20, No. 1, pp. 55–66. doi: 10.1145/225907.225914.

Richards, C. (2004) *Certain to win. The strategy of John Boyd applied to business*. Xlibris Corporation.

Sahal, D. (1979) A theory of evolution of technology. *International Journal of Systems Science*, Vol. 10, No. 3, pp. 259–274.

Schwaber, K. (1995) *Scrum development process, business object design and implementation workshop*. Position Paper. Austin, TX: OOPSLA, 16 October 1995, http://jeffsutherland.org/oopsla/schwaber.html.

Schwaber, K. (1996) Controlled chaos: Living on the edge. *American Programmer*, Vol. 9, No. 4, pp. 11–16.

Schwaber, K. (1997) SCRUM development process. In J. Sutherland, C. Casanave, J. Miller, P. Patel, and G. Hollowell (eds), *Business object design and implementation*. London: Springer-Verlag Limited, pp. 117–134.

Schwaber, K. (2004) *Agile project management with Scrum*. Redmond, WA: Microsoft Press.

Schwaber, K. (2009) *Agile project management with Scrum*. Redmond, WA: Microsoft Press.

Schwaber, K. and Beedle, M. (2002) *Agile software development with SCRUM*. Upper Saddle River, NJ: Prentice Hall.

Senge, P. (1990) *The fifth discipline: The art & practice of the learning organization*. New York: Currency Doubleday.

Sopory, P. and Dillard, J.P. (2002). The persuasive effects of metaphor: A meta-analysis. *Human Communication Research*, Vol. 28, No. 3, pp. 382–419. doi: 10.1111/j.1468-2958.2002.tb00813.x.

Stacey, R. (1993) *Strategic management and organisational dynamics*. London: Pitman Publishing.

Stacey, R. (1996) *Strategic management and organisational dynamics. The challenge of complexity*, 2nd edition. London: Pitman Publishing.

Stacey, R.D. (2000) *Strategic management and organisational dynamics. The challenge of complexity*, 3rd edition. Harlow: Pearson Education Limited.

Stacey, R.D. (2009) *Complexity and organizational reality. Uncertainty and the need to rethink management after the collapse of investment capitalism*. London: Routledge.

Stacey, R.D., Griffin, D. and Shaw, P. (2000) *Complexity and management. Fad or radical challenge to systems thinking*. London and New York: Routledge.

Steen, G. (2008) The paradox of metaphor: Why we need a three-dimensional model of metaphor. *Metaphor and Symbol*, Vol. 23, No. 4, pp. 213–241.

Steen, G. J., Dorst, A. G., Herrmann, J. B., Kaal, A. A., Krennmayr, T., and Pasma, T. (2010) A method for linguistic metaphor identification. From MIP to MIPVU. (Converging Evidence in Language and Communication Research; No. 14). Amsterdam: John Benjamins

Sutherland, J. (2010) *Scrum handbook*. Somerville, MA: Scrum Training Institute Press. https://www.researchgate.net/publication/301685699_Jeff_Sutherland's_Scrum_Handbook.

Sutherland J. (2012). *On Fighter Pilots and Product Owners by Jeff Sutherland*, May 21, Blog, https://www.scruminc.com/on-fighter-pilots-and-product-owners/

Sutherland, J. (2021). *The Scrum Papers: Nuts, Bolts, and Origins of an Agile Framework*, Lincoln MA, https://www.scruminc.com/scrumpapers.pdf

Takeuchi, H. and Nonaka, I. (1986) The new product development game. *Harvard Business Review*, January–February, pp. 137–146.

Waldrop, M.M. (1992) *Complexity: The emerging science at the edge of order and chaos*. New York: Simon & Schuster.

7 Adaptive Software Development and complexity-related ideas

The origins of ASD and complexity: Sources of inspiration

Adaptive Software Development (ASD) grew out of Rapid Application Development (RAD) elaborated in the 1990s by Sam Bayer and Jim Highsmith (Highsmith 2000). The moving force behind this growth was Jim Highsmith, who was fascinated by complexity science (as defined in our typology), and by complex adaptive systems (CAS) in particular. Adaptive Software Development was described in works authored and co-authored by its originator Jim Highsmith (Highsmith 1997, 2000, 2002; Highsmith and Cockburn 2001). The role of complex adaptive systems was reiterated in Highsmith's (2010) book, where a significant extension of Agile beyond project management was proposed.

A different pattern of inspiration of ASD by complexity-related ideas caused a different methodological approach for our study. While in the early stages of Scrum references to complexity and to its related concepts were more general, differentiated, and scattered among several works by its originators, the influence of complexity-related ideas on the origins of ASD was described in a more comprehensive, systematic way. The main reason for such a situation was that ASD was created by a single author deeply inspired by complexity science. In consequence, preparing an extended preliminary inventory of occurrences of the terms relating to complexity in all initial works on ASD was not necessary.

Comprehensive descriptions of ASD presented in the initial works of Highsmith – paper (1997) and books (2000, 2002) – allow the identification of the fundamental sources of knowledge about interpretations of complexity and about akin concepts which lay the groundwork for the development of that Agile methodological framework.

First of all it can be seen that they are very differentiated, beginning from conceptually and mathematically advanced works, e.g. Holland (1995), Kauffman (1993), Langton (edge of chaos) (1989, 1992), and Reynolds (boids) (1987), through the works describing models, associated metaphors and analogies (e.g. Gell-Mann 1994; Kauffman 1995; Arthur 1996; Stacey 1996a), and ending with popular fiction inspired by complexity science (Crichton 1995). Additionally, Highsmith (2000) also refers to the law of requisite variety, a

DOI: 10.4324/9781003175032-8

complexity-related idea from first-order cybernetics (Ashby 1957). Special place in the sources of inspiration of Highsmith is taken by the series of books by Gerald Weinberg devoted to systems thinking and IT. As the representation of the series we quote here the first volume (Weinberg 1991). The list of publications together with brief explanations of their features is given in Table 7.1.

The impact of complex adaptive systems on ASD must be analysed with reference to the environment and the projects. Following the line of reasoning of Highsmith (2000, 2002) in the subsequent part we concentrate on the economic environment of modern projects and on the interpretations of turbulence in management and in project management.

ASD and complex adaptive systems: The economic environment of projects and environmental turbulence

The fundamental universal complexity-related features of the context determining the ideas laying the ground for ASD were initially described in a paper by Highsmith (1997) and, in much extended form, in the book (Highsmith 2000). The article by Brian Arthur, an economist associated with the Santa Fe Institute, published in *Harvard Business Review* (Arthur 1996), was recalled as the first source of inspiration from complexity science in developing ASD. In his paper Arthur explained the change occurring in the economy already in the 1980s and continuing in the 1990s. He wanted to replace in the mainstream economy and in management the old-world view based on traditional industries and technologies dominated by fundamental assumptions of decreasing returns, equilibrium, and deterministic dynamics with the concepts of increasing returns, instability, and the inability to determine cause and effect associated with the knowledge-based economy.

According to Highsmith, the software development community faced a similar dichotomy. The old approach reflected in the more traditional deterministic development, derived from management practices rooted in 19th-century Newtonian physics of stability and predictability – or in Arthur's terms, the economy of diminishing returns – was confronted with a new one, with the economy of increasing returns, in which intangible assets (called incorrectly from the accounting point of view as intellectual capital) and uncertainty play a decisive role. Under new circumstances, businesses shifted from resource-based products to knowledge-based products. In consequence, it became necessary to replace traditional software management practices with new ones – unpredictable, non-linear, and fast.

Environmental turbulence influences all kinds of organizations, and projects. It is mentioned multiple times in Highsmith's (2000, 2002) books as the key environmental factor which contributed to the begetting of ASD and of Agile Project Management, including software development. As already mentioned, in the broadest sense, Agile in management was defined by Highsmith (2002) as adaptation to a turbulent environment. Therefore a recollection of the meaning of turbulence in management and in project management is needed.

Table 7.1 Sources of complexity-related ideas influencing the origins of ASD

Complexity-related concepts	*Sources*
Context of complex adaptive systems in ASD – increasing returns as a determinant of adaptation replacing optimization	Models and metaphors from complexity science (Arthur 1996)
Context of complex adaptive systems in ASD – biological evolution, living company	General interpretations– universal narratives/ metaphors (Wheatley 1992; Johnson 1995; De Geus 1997)
Context and fundamental processes in complex adaptive systems – (organization, innovativeness, leadership)	General interpretations – universal narratives/ metaphors (Bennis and Biedermann 1997)
Complex adaptive systems	Metaphors and models from complexity science (Waldrop 1992; Gell-Mann 1994; Holland 1995, 1998; Stacey 1996a)
Complex adaptive systems and learning	Metaphors and models from complexity science (Holland 1995, 1998)
Emergence, self-organization, learning	Models and metaphors from complexity science (Reynolds 1987 – quoted after Waldrop 1992; Kauffman 1993, 1995; Stacey 1996a)
	Metaphors from complexity science (Coveney and Highfield 1995)
Chaos, edge of chaos	Models from complexity science (Kauffman 1993, 1995)
	Metaphors and models from complexity science (Stacey 1996a)
	Metaphors from complexity science (Waldrop 1992) Langton (no direct source) mentioned after (Waldrop 1992)
	General ideas – metaphors (Crichton 1995)
Misunderstandings of applications of self-organization and chaos theory in management	Metaphors from complexity science (Goldstein 1994)
Chaordic – the concept of Dee Hock	Soft-universal interpretation. Indirect reference to the ideas of Hock (1998)
Systems thinking and understanding complex situations	Systems thinking-based hard and soft interpretations. Reference to the series of books published by Gerald M. Weinberg under the leading title Quality Software Management. (Weinberg 1991)
Systems thinking and learning as a method of understanding complex situations	Systems thinking-based and complexity science-based metaphors (Senge 1990)
Law of requisite variety as a guide in dealing with complexity deriving from variety of environments	Cybernetics-based interpretations of complexity (Ashby 1957)

Sources: Own research based on Highsmith (1997, 2000, 2002).

Etymologically the term turbulence derives from the Latin term *turba* and means commotion, uproar, turmoil, tumult, disturbance, crowd, mob, multitude (Online Etymology Dictionary). From a linguistic perspective, the concept of turbulence in management has been predominantly applied as more or less profoundly defined analogies and metaphors with different meanings.

The history of applications of the term turbulence as describing the state of environment of an organization can be divided into two overlapping areas:

1) Turbulence as a concept of management theory is associated with accelerating dynamics of the company environment and the increasing role of strategic management (Emery and Trist 1965; Ansoff 1965).
2) A broad interpretation describing the dynamic changes of the world proposed in the book *Future Shock* by Toffler (1970) which, together with applications in management, turned out to be relevant to the development of IT, globalization, and especially to the development of the Internet – from the 1970s until the first decade of the 21st century (Ansoff 1979; Drucker 1980; Ansoff *et al.* 2004).

The term turbulent field in management theory was used for the first time by Emery and Trist (1965) to describe the dynamics of an organizational environment. It is interesting to observe that in the self-assessment of the impact of their first paper, Emery (1980) refers to ideas on systems thinking published after 1965 by von Bertalanffy (1968) and Prigogine (1980).

The second concept of a turbulent environment of organizations constitutes one of the core ideas of strategic management developed by (Ansoff 1965, 1979; Ansoff *et al.* 2004). His ideas were also influenced by cybernetics (Ashby 1957) and applications of systems thinking in management (Simon 1957).

In the most recent version of the typology (Ansoff *et al.* 2019) the following are distinguished: (1) Repetitive, (2) expanding (slow incremental), (3) changing (fast incremental), (4) discontinuous (predictable), (5) surprising (discontinuous unpredictable).

The core concept of Ansoff was the Strategic Success Hypothesis also called the Strategic Success Paradigm. According to the most recent version of the Strategic Success Paradigm (Ansoff *et al.* 2019, p. 79), a firm's performance potential is optimum when the following conditions are met:

1) The aggressiveness of the firm's strategic behaviour matches the turbulence of its environment.
2) The responsiveness of the firm's capability matches the aggressiveness of its strategy.
3) The components of the firm's capability must be supportive of one another.
4) The core assumption of the Strategic Success Hypothesis (Strategic Success Paradigm) derives from the law of requisite variety of Ashby (1957, p. 209). Because variety is the measure of complexity, it can be stated that

the complexity and speed of response of the company/projects must match the turbulence of the environment described by the speed of change and complexity.

This introductory example showing the meaning of turbulence illustrates the difficulties which are emerging when a more profound approach is applied in the attempts to define the term Agile and its applications in project management and software development.

References

Ansoff, H.I. (1965) *Corporate strategy – An analytic approach to business policy for growth and expansion*. New York: McGraw-Hill.

Ansoff, H.I. (1979) *Strategic management*. New York: John Wiley & Sons.

Ansoff, H.I., Antoniou, P. and Lewis, A.O. (2004) *Strategic management: Introduction to the Ansoffian approach*. Michigan: Xanedu Press.

Ansoff, H.I., Kipley, D., Lewis, A., Helm-Stevens, R. and Ansoff, R. (2019) *Implanting strategic management*. Cham, Switzerland: Palgrave Macmillan.

Arthur, W.B. (1996) Increasing returns and the two worlds of business. *Harvard Business Review*, Vol. 74, No. 4, pp. 100–109.

Ashby, W.R. (1957) *An introduction to cybernetics*. London: Chapman & Hall.

Bennis, W. and Biederman, P. (1997). *Organizing genius: The secrets of creative collaboration*. Reading, MA: Addison-Wesley Publishing Co.

Coveney, P. and Highfield, R. (1995). *Frontiers of complexity: The search for order in a chaotic world*. New York: Random House/Fawcett Columbine.

Crichton, M. (1995) *The lost world*. New York: Alfred A. Knopf.

De Geus, A. (1997) *The Living Company: Habits for Survival in a Turbulent Business Economy*. Boston: Harvard Business School Press.

Drucker, P.F. (1980) *Managing in turbulent times*. New York: Harper & Row.

Emery, F.E. (1980) This week's citation classic. *CC*, No. 62, pp. 292. https://quotepark.com/authors/fred-emery/?o=popular.

Emery, F.E. and Trist, E.L. (1965) The causal texture of organizational environments. *Human Relations*, Vol. 18, pp. 21–32. doi: 10.1177/001872676501800103.

Gell-Mann, M. (1994) *The quark and the jaguar: Adventures in the simple and the complex*. New York: W.H. Freeman and Company.

Goldstein, J. (1994). *The unshackled organization: Facing the challenge of unpredictability through spontaneous reorganization*. Portland: Productivity Press.

Highsmith, J. (1997) Messy, exciting, and anxiety-ridden: Adaptive software development. *American Programmer*, Vol. 10, No. 1, pp. 23–29.

Highsmith, J.A. III (2000) *Adaptive software development. A collaborative approach to managing complex systems*. New York: Dorset House Publishing Co. (Kindle edition)

Highsmith, J. (2002) *Agile software development ecosystems*. Boston, MA: Addison-Wesley.

Highsmith, J. (2010) *Agile project management*, Second Edition. Creating Innovative Products. Upper Saddle River, NJ: Addison-Wesley (Kindle edition).

Highsmith, J. and Cockburn, A. (2001) Agile software development: The business of innovation. *Computer*, Vol. 34, No. 9, pp. 120–127. doi: 10.1109/2.947100.

Hock, D. (1998) *The birth of the chaordic organization*. New York: Doubleday Business

Holland, J.D. (1995) *Hidden order. How adaptation builds complexity*. New York: Basic Books.

Holland, J.D. (1998) *Emergence: From chaos to order*. Reading, MA: Addison-Wesley.

Johnson, J. (1995). Creating chaos. *American Programmer*, Vol. 8, No. 7, pp. 3–7.

Kauffman, S.A. (1993) *The origins of order: Self-organization and selection in evolution*. New York and Oxford: Oxford University Press.

Kauffman, S.A. (1995) *At home in the universe. The search for laws of self-organization and complexity*. New York and Oxford: Oxford University Press.

Langton, C. G. (1989) Artificial Life, in: C. G. Langton (ed), *Artificial Life: The Proceedings of an Interdisciplinary Workshop on the Synthesis and Simulation of Living Systems. SFI Studies in the Sciences of Complexity, Proceedings, Vol. 6*. Redwood City, CA: Addison-Wesley, pp. 1–48.

Langton, C.G. (1992). Life at the edge of chaos in: C. G. Langton, C. Taylor, J.D. Farmer and S. Rasmussen (eds), *Artificial Life II. Santa Fe Institute Studies in the Sciences of Complexity, Proceedings, vol. 10 (Proceedings of second Artificial Life workshop, 1990)*. Redwood City, CA: Addison-Wesley, pp. 41–91.

Prigogine, I. (1980) *From being to becoming. Time and complexity in the physical sciences*. New York: W. H. Freeman.

Reynolds, C.W. (1987) Flocks, herds, and schools: A distributed behavioral model. *Computer Graphics*, Vol. 21, No. 4, pp. 25–34. doi: 10.1145/37402.37406.

Simon, H.A. (1957) *Administrative behaviour*, 2nd edition. New York: Macmillan.

Stacey, R.D. (1996a) *Complexity and creativity in organizations*. San Francisco, CA: Berrett-Koehler.

Toffler, A. (1970) *Future shock*. New York: Random House.

Von Bertalanffy, L. (1968) *General system theory: Foundations, development, applications*. New York: George Braziller.

Waldrop, M.M. (1992) *Complexity: The emerging science at the edge of order and chaos*. New York: Simon & Schuster.

Weinberg, G. M. (1991) *Quality software management, Vol. 1: Systems Thinking*. New York: Dorset House Publishing.

Wheatley, M J. (1992) *Leadership and the new science: Learning about organizations from an orderly universe*. San Francisco: Berrett-Koehler.

8 Complexity in the Agile Manifesto and in the Declaration of Interdependence

Highsmith and Schwaber claim that the values and principles of the Agile Manifesto were developed under the strong impact of complexity-related ideas. The same conclusion concerns the Declaration of Interdependence.

The already symbolic meeting of 17 software development specialists at Snowbird ski resort in the Wasatch Mountains of Utah from 11 to 13 February 2001, in addition to giving birth to the Agile Alliance, had also another important meaning. For the first time, complexity-related ideas were embedded in the fundamental documents shaping the practice and theory of Agile Project Management – the 4 values of the Manifesto for Agile Software Development (2001) and the 12 principles behind the Manifesto (2001).

According to Highsmith (2002, p. 119), the first value of the Manifesto, prioritizing individuals and interactions over processes and tools, reflects directly the impact of complex adaptive systems (CAS) which constitute the foundations of Adaptive Software Development and play a significant role in Scrum and in other APM approaches.

Freely interacting individuals who are equivalent to agents in CAS can effectively adapt to the changes in an uncertain, turbulent environment. It opens up the possibility of emergence and self-organization, which in turn may lead to greater innovativeness.

The fourth Agile Manifesto value – responding to change postulated over following the plan – also directly mirrors the influence of complexity-related ideas. In some way it signals the adaptive character of software development, allowing the authors to accommodate the perpetual demands of the customer resulting from changes in the environment of the project in the process of its development and subsequent exploitation.

The impact of ideas associated with complexity, and with complex adaptive systems in particular, is also visible in the principles. The second principle: "Welcome changing requirements, even late in development. Agile processes harness change for the customer's competitive advantage" also reflects the need for adaptation to change in the project environment, in the project itself and in the process of developing the projects. Complexity treated in a very general sense was indirectly addressed in the tenth principle: "Simplicity—the art of

DOI: 10.4324/9781003175032-9

maximizing the amount of work not done—is essential". In this case it means that awareness of the complexity of the environment, projects, and processes of development of projects has to lead to reduced complexity and not coping with it by wasting time and resources.

The 11th principle: "The best architectures, requirements, and designs emerge from self-organizing teams" refers to another important topic of complexity-related discourse. Self-organization is exposed not only in the areas of studies openly declaring complexity in their names, e.g. complexity science but also in various areas of cybernetics, systems thinking, etc. As was shown, self-organization also incorporates such issues as the reduction of uncertainty, prediction, adaptation, adaptability, etc.

The impact of broadly defined complexity-related ideas on the origins of the Agile Manifesto and the Agile Alliance can be also identified in another, indirect way. In the process of development of other Agile frameworks of software development, some of the authors were already aware of the characteristics (terminology) of complex adaptive systems. Highsmith (2002, p. 118) states that he, Ken Schwaber, and Kent Beck were likely most familiar with the CAS. It can be illustrated by listing the complexity-related publications of the leading authors of the Agile frameworks. This list includes the following works published before the declaration of the Agile Manifesto: Schwaber (1995, 1996, 1997), Highsmith (1997, 2000).

Complexity and Agile in modern project management: A conceptual framework

The point of departure of the reassessment is summarized in a question: When do we use the term complexity and related notions when applying Scrum in software development? The results depicted in our work provide some new ideas and inspiration for further considerations. As a point of departure the following two-dimensional framework is proposed.

The first dimension refers to the role of observer in developing the interpretations of complexity. It concerns the level of knowledge about all types of complexity and the level of self-reflexivity, not only in general terms but also self-reflexivity concerning the knowledge of complexity of the individuals and teams. The second dimension criterion concerns the variously defined complexity of the project. The main determinants of complexity are the cognitive factors engaged in the functioning of the systems for which software is developed. This dimension is associated with the physical scale of the projects (size, functional complexity, structural complexity). For both criteria a three-level hierarchical typology is developed with full awareness of the limitations of this initial distinction. The proposed concept can be "complexified" in multiple ways, for example, by delving deeper into the physical and cognitive scales of complexity of the projects and of their environment. The complexification may also include linking the physical scale of the projects with consideration of man-machine cognitive interactions.

Table 8.1 The matrix of self-reflexive complexity assessment in software development

		Levels of knowledge about complexity		
		Low – basic knowledge of intuitive complexity and all areas of complexity-related studies (metaphors and mathematical models)	*Medium – knowledge of intuitive complexity and all areas of complexity-related studies (metaphors and mathematical models)*	*High – deep, reflexive and self-reflexive knowledge of main studies of intuitive complexity and of all complexity-related research*
Levels of complexity	**Low** Simple projects not demanding any knowledge of cognition, linguistics, man-machine cognitive relations Independent from the physical scale Potentially complicated projects in a traditional sense	Sufficient for traditional software project development (small- and medium-scale projects)	Useful in some cases for more intricate projects or physical large-scale projects	Unnecessary, redundant
	Medium Projects demanding knowledge of cognition, linguistics, man-machine cognitive relations (text processing, simple AI systems) Large physical scale project Combination of both	Inadequate, partly useful	Fully compatible with the demands of complexity of the project and of its environment	Redundant but can contribute to higher creativity and productivity
	High Projects demanding knowledge of cognition, linguistics, man-machine cognitive relations (advanced text processing, advanced AI systems) Large physical scale projects with significant cognitive elements	Inadequate competences	Insufficient and only partly useful, but can partly contribute to higher productivity	Necessary for all projects belonging to this type, e.g. cognitive systems engineering and/or all types of AI systems

Source: Own research.

The results of scrutiny of the role of complexity and chaos-related vocabulary in all APM allow the development of a framework concept of applications of those terms in modern Scrum and in other methodological frameworks using the term Agile. The preliminary proposal relates not only to software development but may also be directly expanded to other areas of application of Agile methodological frameworks.

The first question we will have to ask in all types of project management is: Why do we use the term complex for the project, environment, and organization developing a project? To provide reasonable answers to this question the following conceptual framework is proposed. It includes two basic dimensions: First, the complexity of the project itself and of its environment, measured with the characteristics of the project and of its environment; and second, the depth of knowledge of interpretations of complexity of the project stakeholders – predominantly customers and authors. As an auxiliary criterion for both dimensions, complexity deriving from the cognitive aspects of projects and their stakeholders is taken into account.

The simple introductory framework embody three levels for each dimension. The examples can be software development or IT system implementation. The first level includes projects which do not demand any engagement with advanced optimization of software, cognitive studies, linguistic analyses, etc. Let's call them typical engineering-like classical projects. The complexity of such projects does not depend on the perceptions and interpretations of the stakeholders. The object (software) is independent of the authors and clients (a typical classical situation of first-order cybernetics).

The second level includes software which demands more advanced semantic studies, preliminary cognitive analyses, e.g. software for text mining.

The third, most advanced level embodies software for advanced systems of artificial intelligence where the cognitive human and machine processes are modelled.

Returning to the initial questions – challenge or fad – it may be stated that applications of metaphors borrowed from complexity theory and chaos theory had the fundamental effect of inspiring practitioners and theoreticians searching for the enrichment of their vocabulary with new, less well-known ideas, e.g. the consequences of non-linearity, the role of self-organization, sensitivity to initial conditions.

As was shown the existing knowledge of how to use the ideas from complexity and chaos theory is insufficient. The reassessment of applications of those ideas in Agile Project Management frameworks should be built upon the following assumptions.

1) Deepened reflection on defining complexity and the characteristics of projects, teams, and environments.
2) The level of awareness of all actors involved in the process of project management. The awareness concerns the complexity of the projects and self-awareness of the project team members.

The example concerns the development of software but it can be extended to other types of projects. As an introduction two three-level typologies are proposed. The first typology refers to the complexity of projects, teams, and environments:

1) Engineering-like projects which are moderately complex (only computational models) with a limited scope of uncertainty and with the need to define the complexity of projects, teams, and environments.
2) Engineering-like projects with the need to include and study the processes of self-organization of teams.
3) Advanced projects in cognitive sciences demanding the preparation of software for man-machine interaction – computable and non-computable characteristics, advanced complex phenomena demanding knowledge of both, and computable and non-computable attributes of complexity.

The second typology describes the level of familiarity with the ideas of complexity – projects, organization, teams:

1) Only intuitive knowledge of characteristics of complexity.
2) Knowledge of characteristics of complexity – intuitive characteristics of complexity and metaphors deriving from complexity and chaos science.
3) Advanced knowledge of all types of complexity and familiarity with advanced problems of man-machine interactions, e.g. artificial intelligence, linguistics.

It is not necessary that each member of the project team is familiar with advanced problems of complex systems. It is only necessary that selected members of team know the advanced complex systems ideas and Agile sufficiently profoundly and they communicate among themselves and with other members of the teams.

As was mentioned in the Introduction, this book includes the preliminary results of our research project. It is a continuous endeavour. Some of the results should be ordered and deepened. The weaknesses of this study will be also eliminated.

The main directions of our future study include:

1. A more profound analysis of the origins of Agile project management.
2. Evolution of Agile project management – scaling, deepening, introduction of advanced methods of applications (man-machine uses) and other specialised approaches.
3. Analysis of the role of reflexivity and self-reflexivity in applying Agile project management in advanced complex projects in software development and in project management in a universal sense.
4. Analysis of the mutual links between Agile project management and agile approaches in business management.

References

Highsmith, J. (1997) Messy, exciting, and anxiety-ridden: Adaptive software development. *American Programmer*, Vol. 10, No. 1, pp. 23–29.

Highsmith, J.A. III (2000) *Adaptive software development. A collaborative approach to managing complex systems*. New York: Dorset House Publishing Co. (Kindle edition)

Highsmith, J. (2002) *Agile software development ecosystems*. Boston, MA: Addison-Wesley.

Manifesto for Agile Software Development (2001) http://agilemanifesto.org/

Principles behind the Agile Manifesto (2001) http://agilemanifesto.org/principles.html

Schwaber, K. (1995) SCRUM development process. http://www.jeffsutherland.org/oopsla/schwapub.pdf

Schwaber, K. (1996) Controlled chaos: Living on the edge. *American Programmer*, Vol. 9, No. 4, pp. 11–16.

Schwaber, K. (1997) SCRUM development process. In J. Sutherland, C. Casanave, J. Miller, P. Patel, and G. Hollowell (eds.), *Business object design and implementation*. London: Springer-Verlag Limited, pp. 117–134.

Index

For Product Safety Concerns and Information please contact our EU representative GPSR@taylorandfrancis.com
Taylor & Francis Verlag GmbH, Kaufingerstraße 24, 80331 München, Germany

www.ingramcontent.com/pod-product-compliance
Ingram Content Group UK Ltd.
Pitfield, Milton Keynes, MK11 3LW, UK
UKHW022355190926
475702UK00015B/2312

* 9 7 8 1 0 3 2 0 0 6 5 4 3 *